QUEST

Teacher's Book

GABRIELLA LAZZERI **3** STEVE MARSLAND

LONGMAN

Pearson Education Limited,
Edinburgh Gate, Harlow,
Essex CM20 2JE, England
and Associated Companies throughout the world.

First published 1999
Set in Berkeley, Eurocrat and Stone Sans

Printed in Spain by Mateu Cromo

ISBN 0 582 31641 3

Cover illustration by Roberto Bertolini.

Illustrations by Roberto Bertolini, Linzi Henry and Chris Pavely.

Author Acknowledgements:
Quest is dedicated to our respective families; to Mary, Iole,
Manuela and Daniele; to the memory of Athos Lazzeri and
John Marsland, who introduced us to the world of
storytelling, and to Athos, Alessandro, Debora, John and
David who have shared in the adventure.

Find Longman ELT on http://www.awl-elt.com

CONTENTS

CONTENTS MAP

UNIT 0	Lesson 1	Lesson 2
Objectives	To re-establish contact with English	To re-establish contact with English
Target Language	Revision of language from *Quest 1* and *Quest 2*	Revision of language from *Quest 1* and *Quest 2*

UNIT 1	Lesson 1	Lesson 2	Lesson 3	Lesson 4
Objectives	To identify the planets in our solar system by their names and simple descriptions	To compare physical features	To develop reading comprehension skills To discover information about the solar system	To talk about life in space To express reason and desire to do something To develop reading skills
Target Language	Planets *moon, planet, rings, solar system, space, spaceship, spot, star, sun*	Comparatives and superlatives	Superlatives Measurements *volcano, ocean, twin, whale*	*want* + infinitive

UNIT 2	Lesson 1	Lesson 2	Lesson 3	Lesson 4	Lesson 5
Objectives	To ask about, suggest and choose means of transport	To identify places in town and ask for/give information	To identify points of the compass To ask for/give directions about where you live	To be able to read a map To ask for/give directions	To find out about places in London
Target Language	*How do you get to ...? Let's go by ..., on foot*	Places in town	Points of the compass *city, town, village Where do you live?*	Directions *street, road, building*	Places in London

UNIT 3	Lesson 1	Lesson 2	Lesson 3	Lesson 4
Objectives	To ask for, give and justify opinions	To ask about a scene and give a description (1)	To ask about a scene and give a description (2)	To ask about a scene and give a description (3); to build a narrative
Target Language	*What do you think it is/ they are? Why? I think it's a/they are ... because ...*	Language of description	Language of description	Language of description and narrative

UNIT 4	Revision Unit

UNIT 5	Lesson 1	Lesson 2	Lesson 3	Lesson 4
Objectives	To discover new currencies To handle prices, coins and banknotes	To identify toys and games To ask for something To ask about/give prices for toys and games	To talk about shops and items sold To distinguish between countable and uncountable nouns	To describe how to get to places To find out about famous British shops
Target Language	English and American currency *coins, banknotes, money*	*Can I help you? I'd like a/some ..., please. Here you are. How much is it?* Toys *a/an, some*	Shops Food Holidays *need*	Shops *go past, along*

UNIT 6	Lesson 1	Lesson 2	Lesson 3	Lesson 4
Objectives	To make suggestions and accept/refuse them	To talk about camping	To talk about camping activities To describe what is happening/what people are doing	To learn about National Parks To stimulate environmental awareness
Target Language	*What shall we do? Let's ...* *Me too.*	Camping equipment	Camping activities	Animals

UNIT 7	Lesson 1	Lesson 2	Lesson 3	Lesson 4
Objectives	To ask for things To ask for clarification	To describe objects To give explanations To develop listening skills	To identify jobs and describe what people do	To ask about jobs and describe what people do
Target Language	Equipment *Can you give me ...?* *Which one(s)? The (red).* *one(s).*	*Which one do you want?*	*What's his/her job?* *S/He's a ...* Jobs Present Simple tense *outside/inside, during the day/at night* *van*	*Does he/she ...? Yes, he/she does./No, he/she doesn't.*

UNIT 8	Revision Unit

UNIT 9	Lesson 1	Lesson 2	Lesson 3	Lesson 4
Objectives	To say what you are afraid of and why To agree	To find out about and describe animal habits	To describe routines and habits To express degrees of frequency	To discover information To ask about habits Consolidation of *do* as auxiliary verb
Target Language	*I'm afraid of ... the dark, water, spiders, mice, bees* *dirty, hairy, slimy* *fly, sting, bite*	*Does it ...? / Is it ...?*	Present Simple tense	*Do you?*

UNIT 10	Lesson 1	Lesson 2	Lesson 3	Lesson 4
Objectives	To describe and give instructions for movement	To talk about rules and regulations	To talk about rules and regulations To explain a route to follow	To talk about the past To say where you were and ask where other people were
Target Language	Prepositions of movement	*must/mustn't*	*must/mustn't* *wall, rock*	*I was ... .* *Where were you?*

UNIT 11	Lesson 1	Lesson 2	Lesson 3	Lesson 4
Objectives	To ask and talk about people's intentions	To talk about holiday plans	To discriminate between descriptions To recognise the use of emphasis	To make/accept/reject suggestions To talk about films and videos
Target Language	*What are you going to be?* *I'm going to be a ...* Jobs *famous*	*Where?/How?/What are you going to ...?* Holidays	Descriptions of people	*What shall we do/watch?* *Let's watch ...* Types of film

UNIT 12	Revision Unit

INTRODUCTION

Course overview

What is *Quest* and who is it for?

Quest is a story-based course for young children who are studying English at primary school. *Quest* presents English through a story and so provides an exciting alternative to traditional coursebooks for pupils and teacher alike. Each of the three levels of the course uses a highly stimulating adventure story to contextualise the target language. *Quest* is suitable for teachers with many years of experience of teaching English to primary schoolchildren as well as for those who are teaching the subject for the first time. This is because *Quest* has been written by teachers for teachers bearing in mind both the need for guidance and options for creativity. *Quest* has been specifically designed to meet the needs of young learners as it satisfies their need for adventure and challenge while giving them enjoyable and achievable tasks.

How many hours does *Quest* provide?

Quest aims to set teaching objectives that are realistic and also provide variety and flexibility. The course provides 90–100 hours of classroom material, but as teaching schedules and the length of lessons vary, the course also includes a wide range of extra activities which allows the core material to be extended to meet individual needs.

How is the material in *Quest* organised?

Each level of *Quest* consists of a Student's Book, a Teacher's Book and a set of two class cassettes. There are twelve units in each level of *Quest* – nine main units which contain an episode of the adventure story followed by language presentation and practice, and three Revision Units. The first four pages of each main unit in the Student's Book contain an episode of the adventure story which contextualises the target language through stimulating illustrations and evocative sound effects. The remaining pages of each main unit are dedicated to the presentation and practice of the target language through a wealth of activities including games, songs, projects and cross-curricular material. There is a magazine-style page in some units which highlights aspects of life in the countries where English is used.

The Teacher's Book contains easy-to-use notes on all the activities in the Student's Book and suggestions for a wide range of additional activities. There is also a photocopiable resource section at the back of the Teacher's Book (see page 16 for more information on the features in the Teacher's Book).

The cassettes contain recordings of all the episodes of the adventure story, the *Listen and repeat* language models, activities for intensive and extensive listening practice, and all the songs, raps and chants included in the course.

What methodology is *Quest* based on?

The material in *Quest* has been carefully developed to reflect the needs and interests of young learners, and the methodology which underlies the material aims to take full advantage of children's amazing ability to learn through experience and emotion.

The key aspects of the methodology are as follows:

- **a carefully graded syllabus.** The language in *Quest* has been selected for its relevance to young learners and it has been graded to be presented in a logical order and in manageable amounts.
- **the careful contextualisation of target language through the episodes of the adventure story**. This helps the children to understand the language in a context which is motivating and memorable.
- **the clear highlighting of target language through *Listen and repeat* activities.** These activities mark the beginning of a new language focus in the material. Where possible, they present the target language in the visual context in which it was first seen in the story and so help the children to identify with the language. They include amounts of language that children will find manageable and they also provide a pronunciation model for the initial production of the target structure, function or lexis. This allows the children to focus on a small section of the story dialogue and so reduces the possibility of language overload.
- **the inclusion of carefully controlled practice leading to personalisation.** The *Listen and repeat* activities provide initial controlled practice of the target language. The activities that follow encourage progressively freer practice and personalisation. Getting the children to use the language to talk about their own lives, the lives of people around them and the world in which they live is an important stage in the learning process.
- **the staging of activities.** *Quest* follows a pattern in the staging of the activities which allows the children to deal with the target language in a

manageable way – they listen before they speak, they speak before they read, and they read before they write. This approach allows the children to hear, identify and understand the target language before they produce it orally. Then they repeat and practise it in speaking activities before being asked to recognise the written form. The final stage is for them to produce the written form themselves.

- **the staging and development of skills.** *Quest* contains activities that practise all learning skills. However, it does not follow a fixed sequence of skills, as the choice and amount of skills practice needed varies with the target language. There is an emphasis on the development of listening and speaking skills, although there are short reading texts which serve as a model for simple writing activities. *Quest* 3 develops these skills by providing activities to encourage narrative writing.

- **constant revision and recycling.** Giving the children the opportunity to repeat the language they have covered in earlier units and reuse it in a different context is very important in the learning process. The material in *Quest* provides regular Revision Units in the Student's Book, and the notes in the Teacher's Book provide suggestions for recycling language across the lessons and units.

- **a variety of activity types.** As different target language lends itself to different forms of practice, *Quest* contains a wide variety of activities selected to suit the language. These are based on a 'learning by doing' approach (task-based activities, simple experiments, TPR (Total Physical Response) activities, etc.). This range of activities provides variety and pace in the lessons and so helps to prevent the children becoming bored or overexcited.

- **cooperative learning.** Learning to work together is an important skill, not only in the English classroom but also in all aspects of school life. Many of the activities in *Quest* help to promote cooperation and collaboration among the children. There are activities which are specifically designed to be carried out in pairs or groups and also suggestions in the Teacher's Book for making the setting up of activities and the production of materials into a collaborative process.

- **the importance of the classroom as the children's learning environment.** Unlike adults, children will have comparatively little opportunity to use English outside the classroom. It is therefore very important to use English in the communicative situations that exist in the classroom, e.g. giving instructions,

giving feedback and praise, maintaining discipline, etc. The classroom language which was systematically introduced in *Quest* 1 and 2 should continue to be used, and added to, by the teacher in order to ensure that English is the main language of classroom communication.

- **cross-cultural content.** *Quest* includes material which highlights aspects of life and culture of the countries where English is used. This material is presented through images and recordings of English-speaking children and adults and encourages the children using the material to make comparisons with their own life and culture. The Teacher's Book provides background information to this material.

- **cross-curricular content.** As children are not learning English in isolation, it can be productive to draw on aspects of other school subjects, e.g. Maths, Music, Art, Geography, etc. This helps the children to see their learning in an integrated way and also provides variety.

The *Quest* approach

The material in *Quest* is organised around a highly motivating adventure story, which serves as a point of departure for the majority of the lessons. For many teachers the use of stories in the classroom may be new or storytelling sessions may be seen as just an additional activity to be included in some lessons. There is, however, strong justification for integrating stories into children's learning in a systematic way. Children often have difficulty in remembering exactly what they were doing at a certain time or place, yet can remember incredible details from stories they heard when they were younger. Stories involve a succession of events linked by a logical explanation – a feature that helps children to focus their attention accurately. By presenting language through a narrative, the language becomes one of the details to be remembered. The excitement aroused when listening to a story heightens receptivity and reinforces the impact of the story on the memory. If the children feel motivated and enjoy the way in which language is presented to them, they are much more likely to remember the language itself.

The key features of the *Quest* approach are:

a the story

The exciting adventure story in each level involves characters and situations with which the children will

INTRODUCTION

identify. The story format ensures both continuity and contextualisation as the children follow the characters on their adventures. The story is not only the vehicle by which the target language is introduced and contextualised but also serves as a thematic link throughout the course.

The main objectives of each episode of the story are:
- to contextualise language items in a stimulating and challenging way.
- to help the children to identify the characters and situations.
- to stimulate the children's involvement in the story.
- to develop the children's listening skills.
- to revise previously learnt language and use it in a different context.

The story provides ample scope for drama and roleplay activities, artwork and handicraft activities and also represents a ready-made revision tool.

b the story-linked presentation

Giving children a story-linked presentation of language takes advantage of the stimulation and enthusiasm generated by the story. Once the children have followed the episode of the story and are familiar with the events, a 'flashback' to a particular scene is used to focus their attention on the context, the functional aspect of the utterance and the language produced to carry out the function effectively. The 'flashbacks' are a vivid way of isolating the language without losing the contextualisation which the children hold in their memory. With conventional presentations where the language is presented via a situation, the children are often distracted by the details in the illustrations and are more anxious to focus on the situation and the characters than on the language.

c thematic guided practice

Thematic guided practice is the first step in the gradual process of extending the story-linked presentation. Once the language item has been presented and the children have been given initial pronunciation and intonation practice, Quest takes the children through a logical extension of the language moving systematically from the adventure story to a broader context. The practice material provided in Quest covers a wide variety of individual, pair and group activities and the emphasis is on maintaining the challenge and enjoyment present in the story. The tasks are carefully graded to include previously taught language items in order to integrate the unfamiliar with the familiar. There are ideas and suggestions in the Teacher's Book for increasing the challenge element in the activities should the teacher want to cater for a more demanding class.

d real-life contexts and personalisation

Real-life contexts and personalisation take the children one step further with the language. They can now handle the mechanics of the new language and have practised it in controlled activities. The next step is to apply the language in a context which is meaningful to the children's own life and experience. School life and the classroom are the predominant features of the children's real world and so what happens during English lessons is not simply a simulated experience – classroom organisation and routines are meaningful. The syllabus in Quest recognises this and as a result the most immediate extended context for the new language items is often classroom-based. The language is also seen as meaningful to the children if it allows them to achieve an aim or carry out a task. This language may be used in the setting up of a game or a mingling activity or in learning and singing a song.

e cross-cultural awareness

Quest aims to highlight the presence of the English language in the lives of non-native children. Young learners are in contact with English from a wide range of sources and they want to know about the words that they come across in pop songs, in children's TV programmes, advertising and in the products they buy. The Culture Vulture sections in Quest provide the teacher with a framework for focusing on aspects of life and culture of the countries where English is used. These magazine-style pages aim to stimulate and motivate the children in order to foster a positive attitude towards the language. So that the children can understand and enjoy these sections, guided activities are provided as part of the core material. A certain amount of the interaction based on these pages will need to be done in the children's own language. Teachers should not feel worried or guilty about this as the Culture Vulture pages also serve to satisfy the children's curiosity and help them compare and contrast their own experience of the world presented in these pages. The Culture Vulture sections provide for discussion in the children's own language and these moments of interaction between the teacher and the children are as important to the overall development of the children's education as the presentation and practice of new language items (see page 16 for more information on the *Culture Vulture* pages).

There is a wide range of activities included in *Quest* that appeal to the children's own experience and opinions. These include projects, wall charts, surveys and cross-curricular activities. The Teacher's Book has been designed to provide background information and hints on how to extend and develop the core material in an area of particular interest.

f attention to children's learning strategies

Teachers often remark on how well children perform during the lesson but how little they manage to recall at a later date. Children see the language they learn as closely linked to a particular lesson and are often unable to manipulate the language outside that environment. This means that once the teacher moves on from the target language, it will be quickly forgotten unless regularly revised.

The role of association in the learning process is fundamental – a given phrase or utterance learnt within a specific context is unlikely to be freely applied to parallel situations no matter how appropriate the context may be. When children fail to apply the language item, it is often assumed that they are unable to recall it due to poor memory. When children communicate in their own language, however, it is clear that most of them have a formidable memory. When some minor detail is overlooked when recapping on an event or returning to a subject, children can be relied upon to supply the detail, yet they have difficulty recalling a simple question like *Have you got a dog?* when asked to do so. Children need reference points and associations to be able to take advantage of their agile memories. They need to be able to recognise the need for a language item that was presented in a different context in the present situation. A narrative-based approach has several advantages in helping the young learner to broaden associations and extend the use of a particular structure. The story fuses various contexts together and provides a line of events along which the teacher can run backwards and forwards encouraging the children to produce context-linked language. Using episodes from a familiar story to illustrate parallel contexts saves time – the environments are familiar, and the ideas and emotions expressed are there just as the children left them. With a few words the teacher can recreate a scene and its contextualised language item. By encouraging the children to switch

from scene to scene and to become aware of the similarity in the language required in each, they will gradually develop the ability to seek out parallel contexts. The recycling of language in the story in slightly different contexts, constant consolidation and varying questioning techniques will slowly change the children's context-bound approach to language learning.

Using the story in class
Story time

The effectiveness of storytelling as a communicative tool depends on the storyteller's ability to transmit the atmosphere, drama, tension and humour to the listener. In order to help the teacher achieve this, the storyline in *Quest* is supported by attractive and stimulating drawings to illustrate the story and strong audio contextualisation.

Listening to stories is in some ways an intimate moment and one in which the children's receptive senses are very finely tuned. The rapport between the teacher and the children is therefore very important in *Story time* sessions. One key factor is to allow ample time for the children to follow and enjoy the story. Some teachers have experience of using stories, while for others it is a new and possibly daunting addition to their teaching repertoire. The section that follows provides overall guidelines for all teachers on setting up and managing each *Story time* session. The Teacher's Book contains further notes which are specific to each episode of the story.

1 Setting up the *Story time* session

Make sure all the children can see you and that you can make eye contact with all of them. Look at different children while talking to them, as this will make them feel more involved in the events of the story. Your facial expressions will also help to convey your reactions to what is happening in the story, so make sure your expressions and gestures are visible to the whole class.

Before starting the story itself, it is wise (particularly with younger learners) to see if anybody needs anything, e.g. to go to the toilet, to take off or put on a pullover, to blow his/her nose, etc. This helps to avoid distractions during the *Story time* session and also helps to mark the beginning of the session as a special time.

Try to use as many familiar English words and simple structures as possible when setting up the *Story time* sessions.

INTRODUCTION

2 Reviewing the story so far

Apart from when dealing with the first episode, elicit from the class what has happened in the story so far. During these warm-up sessions, try to ask the children as many questions as possible in English using simple questions that they have already met like *Who's this? What's this? What colour is it? Where is (Kanda)?* etc. As the course progresses, you will gradually be able to use more and more English in this initial stage.

Keep the children interested and involved by recapping on key language and events from the previous unit. As the course progresses, involve the children more in recapping by getting them to repeat selected parts of the dialogues from previous episodes.

3 Setting the scene

Focus attention on the first frame in the episode and get the children to describe the scene in their own language. Expand and echo their answers in English to help them set the scene in an English framework.

4 Prediction

Focus attention on the illustrations for the episode. Ask the children what they think the key characters will do next, e.g. how will (Ben) overcome an obstacle or solve a problem that presented itself at the end of the previous episode. Accept all answers with curiosity for the moment, giving no indication as to whether the children have guessed correctly.

5 Observation

Much of the narrative in *Quest* is conveyed by the images as much as by the recording. Let the children have a few minutes to look at the other frames in the episode and see for themselves what happens. This is a crucial stage in that it allows you to focus attention on specific scenes and situations, to establish context and an accurate perception of what is taking place and what is being said from a functional point of view. (Refer to the notes for individual *Story time* sessions for a list of things to check in each episode.) Encourage the children to ignore the speech bubbles at this stage and to focus on the content of the illustrations and what is taking place. If appropriate, let the children read through the previous episode to enable them to refresh their memory with the written word, too. Resist the temptation to answer detailed questions about the story at this point.

6 First listening

Tell the children they are going to listen to the next episode in the story and as they do so, they should follow the frames with their fingers. The point at which the children should move from one frame to another is recorded as a sound effect on the tape. Make sure the children recognise and can respond to it by playing the first few frames of the first episode and demonstrating the activity. While the children listen and follow, move around the class and check that all the children are moving from frame to frame at the correct points.

7 Subsequent listening(s)

If you feel the children need to listen again, particularly with later units containing more language and faster action, play the story again pausing the tape at the crucial moments in the story. Check that the children have understood by asking questions, e.g. *What's the problem here? What's that (noise)? Where are they now?* etc.

8 Focused listening

Once the children have a general understanding of the episode, set them some focus questions. These questions provide a reason for subsequent listening(s) and highlight the key language in the episode. (Refer to the notes for individual *Story time* sessions for a list of things the children need to listen for.)

9 Final note

Before moving on to the presentation stage, it is important that you are confident the children have understood what is happening but not necessarily what the characters are saying literally. Remember to recap on the key events of the story to set the scene for the language presentation.

As a further activity, you can also assign one of the characters to a small group of children and get them to listen and repeat while trying to imitate the voice of the character. Do not focus on the language content at this stage; the imitation is simply to create involvement, and to reinforce the good/evil roles of the main characters.

Further uses of the story

Drama time

Drama time provides the children with an opportunity to act out the story and so provides the teacher with an entertaining and flexible recycling tool. The *Drama time* session comes at the end of each unit that has an episode of the story and it can be done as a quick roleplay of the episode or extended to be a full dramatisation. (*Drama time* is also the name for other dramatisation activities which appear at different points in the teacher's notes and may or may not be based on the story characters.)

Having the *Drama time* session at the end of each unit allows the teacher and children to take full advantage of the practice activities which have consolidated the target language. The children are encouraged to act out the scenes from an episode (or more than one episode) together with the story dialogues. The children get systematic practice of the target language throughout the unit, many of the passive language items in the story are activated through classroom language and the remaining language can be dealt with as 'disposable' language that does not need to be presented.

If you wish to make the session more challenging, you could add an episode each time so that the children act out two or three episodes in each *Drama time* session.

1 Grouping the children

Divide the class into small groups so that there are enough children for each of the characters in the episode (including Jasper). Decide if you want each child to choose his/her role or if it is better to assign a role to each child based on personality and capabilities. It is advisable to vary the groups for each *Drama time* session so that certain students do not always dominate.

2 Preparation

Get the children to listen to the episode of the story again and follow in their books. Classroom space permitting, each group should ideally have a corner in which to prepare its performance. Get them to rehearse by going through the story in their groups with each child saying the lines relating to his/her character. While they are rehearsing, go round helping anyone who is having difficulty.

Once the children are confident about what to say, they should decide what dramatisation techniques they are going to add, e.g. miming actions and movements, pointing while speaking, facial expressions and gestures, etc.

3 Acting out the episode

Get each group to act out the episode at the front of the classroom or where there is most space available. When the last group has finished, the class can then

decide which they felt was the best performance. Make sure the children understand that 'the best' may not necessarily be the one which most closely resembled the original story and may not be the one in which the language of the episode was reproduced most accurately.

4 Follow up

The children could finish the *Drama time* session with the song, chant or rap that they prefer from the unit.

5 Alternative exploitation

An alternative option is to assign different scenes within the episode to different groups or for each group to choose the scene from the episode they prefer and to act out just that part.

Storyboard

The *Storyboard* activities appear in the Revision Units 4, 8 and 12 and they cover the episodes of the story that precede these units. The *Storyboard* provides the children with another way of reusing the story and recycling key language. In each *Storyboard* session, the children create a section of a wall frieze showing the main scenes from the relevant section of the story. The children work in groups and draw the scenes and speech bubbles for the main action. They can refer back to their books but straight copying should be discouraged. A certain amount of creativity in reinterpreting the images and dialogues should be encouraged.

Project work and other activities

The story in each level of *Quest* can be used as a springboard for a range of other projects and activities. This includes the children making individual picture books based on the story, writing their own picture stories based on *Quest* characters or new characters, creating posters and puppets of the characters, drawing other parts of the story settings, e.g. other sections of Rui's spaceship, other sources of the three materials needed, other areas of the maps, etc. Other activities include spotting the mistake in acting or telling an episode of the story with the children including themselves as one of the characters, putting the frames from the story into the correct order, miming and guessing a character, interviewing a character, etc.

INTRODUCTION

The syllabus

Needs analysis is an essential feature in syllabus design. A frequent criticism is that syllabus design for children merely adopts simplified adult learning programmes which are based on adult language requirements. For this reason, the syllabus in *Quest* has been devised to focus primarily on the needs and interests of the child across the three levels. *Quest* 1 allows the child to talk mainly about himself/herself, *Quest* 2 allows the child to talk about himself/herself and others and *Quest* 3 allows the child to talk about the world around him/her.

The story provides a framework that contextualises the following key aspects of the syllabus: functions, e.g. talking about positions and location; structures, e.g. *How do you get to ...?*; topics and lexis, e.g. toys and games; notions, e.g. space and time; and skills, e.g. listening for key information, recording information, etc.

The story gives a clear contextualisation of the target language in a meaningful and memorable way and also provides a vehicle for previewing certain language items. This language is explained during the *Story time* sessions but is not presented or practised until later in the course. When this language item is presented and practised, the children will already be familiar with it and so be more receptive to using it in an active way. This approach also encourages stress-free learning and reduces the possibility of language overload. The functional, structural and lexical aspects of the syllabus are introduced by the regular *Listen and repeat* activities, which mark the start of a new language cycle. These activities highlight the phonological aspects of the target language and let the children practise the language in a non-threatening situation before moving on to initial controlled practice and then freer practice.

The syllabus in *Quest* provides for the recycling of target language across the episodes of the story itself and also in the activities in the Student's Book and in the Teacher's Book. *Quest* also includes three specially written Revision Units which provide regular consolidation of the language presented in the previous units. The revision material provides a wide range of activities based on the characters and themes in the story and also on new characters and situations. The Revision Units cover all four skills and bring together the language from previous units in enjoyable formats such as board games, songs and project work. Two important aspects in revision and consolidation are the *Drama time* and *Storyboard* features which allow the children to recapture the most exciting moments of the story (see pages 10 and 11 for more information on *Drama time* and *Storyboard*).

The syllabus in *Quest* includes a strong classroom language sub-syllabus which takes advantage of the real environment in which the children see a need to communicate in English. Everything that happens in the classroom is a part of the children's real world of English – taking out books, moving chairs and desks, tidying up, leaving the room, organising and taking part in games and activities are all meaningful and relevant to the children's everyday life. For this reason *Quest* places a strong emphasis on allowing the children to perform these tasks in English, and so classroom language assumes great importance in the syllabus. The close association between classroom language and the syllabus ensures that language recycling is done in a meaningful and visual way with the children gradually extending the contexts in which the language items can be used.

The Student's Book
The structure of *Quest*

There are twelve units in each level of *Quest*, nine of which are dedicated to the development of the story and the presentation, practice and recycling of language items. The three remaining Revision Units give the children the opportunity to review and consolidate previously presented structure and lexis in a different context. The Revision Units also provide the teacher with the opportunity to check on the progress being made by using the revision activities as testing material.

The nine story units consist of four pages for the story and the remaining pages for the practice activities. (Unit 7 has five practice pages.) With the exception of Unit 2, which includes teaching material for five lessons, each story unit is designed to be dealt with over four classroom lessons with each unit starting with the *Story time* session.

The Revision Units consist of one or two pages and are designed to be dealt with over two lessons. Each level of *Quest* provides 90–100 hours of classroom time. This is only a guideline and one of the key features in *Quest* is the flexibility of the material which means that the teacher can supplement the material in the Student's Book with a range of extra activities contained in the Teacher's Book (see page 16 for more information on the Teacher's Book).

The icons in the Student's Book

Quest uses a series of icons in the Student's Book and Teacher's Book to highlight what kind of activity is taking place. The icons that appear in the Student's Book also appear in the Teacher's Book but there are some icons which appear in the Teacher's Book only (see page 16). The icons which appear in the Student's Book are:

 indicates a song, rap or chant

 indicates a game

 indicates a project or handicraft activity

 indicates a *Culture Vulture* page

The structure of the story units

The first contact the children have with the target language is through the story on the first four pages of the unit (see page 9 for more information on the *Story time* sessions). The language is then presented via a 'flashback' presentation in the *Listen and repeat* activities and used in initial controlled practice and then freer practice in the following six pages of activities. These include TPR (Total Physical Response) activities such as games, movement to music and physical participation; songs, chants and raps; and a range of activities based on visual stimuli, aural skills, other subjects in the school curriculum and learning strategies. See below for the structure of the units in diagram form. This sequence is repeated for the remaining language cycles in a unit.

Listen and repeat activities

1 Setting the scene for the 'flashback' presentation

Before presenting new language in a *Listen and repeat* activity via a 'flashback' to the story, it is important to set the scene so that the children can concentrate on the context and be receptive to the input. Set the scene by reminding the students of the relevant section of the story. You will find specific scene-setting instructions and context-building hints in the relevant sections of the Teacher's Book.

2 Focusing on the 'flashback' scene(s)

Get the children to look at the 'flashback' scene(s) which is usually a frame or frames taken or adapted from the story. Check that the children understand the context of the scene by asking the children in L1 what they think is going to be said.

3 The *Listen and repeat* stage

All the target language in the speech bubbles of the *Listen and repeat* activities is recorded on tape. Many of the items are taken directly from the story and are contextualised in exciting moments in the narrative. This provides the teacher with the target language in an easily accessible form and also gives a clear pronunciation model for the children to follow. Systematic repetition helps the children to recognise and reproduce unfamiliar sounds and establishes natural intonation patterns. It also serves as a confidence-builder in letting the children hear themselves producing the language in a 'non-challenging'

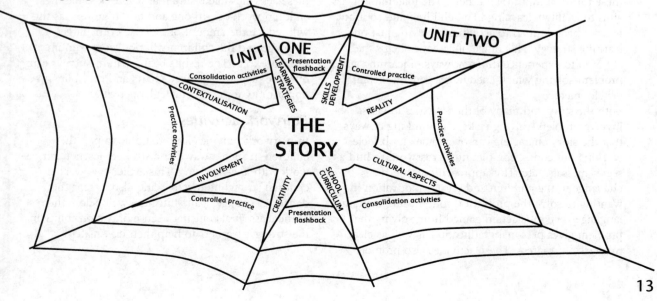

situation, i.e. without the distraction of having to concentrate simultaneously on another task.

Encourage the children to imitate the sounds and intonation in the model as closely as possible. Get the children to listen to the model and repeat it chorally several times. This allows the children to have a chance to reproduce the language as a whole class and so takes away the stress of saying the words out loud individually. Once the children have reproduced the model as a whole class, get them to repeat it in small groups and then individually. If the target language consists of a question and answer, get the children to reproduce the language as an exchange with one child producing the question and another responding.

4 Initial controlled practice

After the presentation of the target language in the *Listen and repeat* stage, the children need to be given the opportunity to use the language in a controlled practice phase. This helps them to manipulate the language with the help of the teacher in a stress-free way. Notes on how to set up initial controlled practice are provided in the relevant sections of the Teacher's Book. The techniques used include cueing sentences with flashcards and classroom objects, eliciting true sentences, using the pictures in the Student's Book to set up question and answer practice, etc.

Practice activities

Quest includes a variety of activity types which cater for the different ways in which children learn – through sight, sound, touch, physical sensations and movement and via a process of association and deduction. Some children are more sensitive to one of these forms of input than others. The material in *Quest* aims to facilitate learning in all children and so input has not been limited to activities involving just one learning strategy. This range of activities helps the children to experience different ways of learning and problem-solving which encourages general mental development.

Both the story and many of the activities in *Quest* involve problem-solving tasks, e.g. thinking of ways that the story characters can overcome an obstacle, working out codes, completing a crossword to find a secret message, etc. This approach presents a challenge to the children and creates motivation in wanting to solve the problem through using the target language. The satisfaction gained from solving the problem gives personal gratification as well as clear markers of progress. These activities also promote collaboration, consultation and mutual help through pairwork, groupwork and teamwork.

Great emphasis has been placed on developing listening skills. *Quest* provides carefully graded activities which guide the learners through a wide variety of extensive and intensive listening tasks designed to develop global and specific understanding. Much of the material in *Quest* is of cross-curricular interest in the subject matter and also in the type of activity involved and the skills practised. These activities can lead to collaboration with teachers of other subjects and so the English lessons not only improve the children's linguistic competence but also contribute to their overall educational development.

Patterns of interaction

The activities in *Quest* are designed to promote different patterns of interaction – activities with the whole class, pairwork and individual work.

Activities with the whole class

When the children are involved in a problem-solving activity, it is advisable not to reveal the solution until all the children have finished. This helps to keep the children's interest throughout the activity and also gives the slower learners a chance to finish without being told the solution. While the faster learners are waiting, give them a short activity to do, e.g. read through a story produced earlier in class, look back at an earlier activity in the book and try it again, read the last story episode, etc.

Quest includes a number of mingling activities where the children have to complete tables and charts with information collected from their classmates. During these activities make sure that where possible the children work one-to-one and not in groups, as this will reduce the amount of practice of the target language and the children will not get maximum exposure to it. The results of these mini-surveys can often be displayed on wall charts and they offer an opportunity for cross-curricular activities.

Pairwork activities

In pairwork activities it is advisable to pair the children in such a way that a stronger learner can work with a weaker one. This avoids two weaker children struggling together and also lessens the danger of stronger pairs finishing well before the rest of the class. It also instils a sense of responsibility in the stronger learners to help their classmates.

Individual work

The activities that involve the children working on their own allow them the space to express themselves without being influenced by their partners or other classmates. The checking phase at the end of an activity can be done as a competition using a points system. Alternatively, the children can simply exchange books, check their partner's answers, point out any mistakes and get their partners to correct them.

Games

Quest includes a wide variety of games, all of which have a clear linguistic objective. These include guessing games, action games, vocabulary games, board games, miming games, TPR games and quizzes. Games are an excellent way of getting the children to feel less constrained by the classroom environment and so freer to express themselves. They allow the teacher to change the pace of the lesson, extend the range of activities and so introduce variety and enjoyment into the lesson. Children need frequent changes in pace and activity type to avoid a loss in their concentration. The games that involve TPR allow the children to demonstrate understanding without having to use language. They also help the children get rid of excess energy and so reduce the possibility of the children fidgeting in later activities.

The games in *Quest* can be played more than once either for revision purposes or whenever a change of pace is needed. Games that involve the teacher may be played again with one of the children taking the teacher's role.

Hints on using games

Read the Teacher's Book carefully before starting a game and check that you have the necessary space and equipment (if required). If the game you want the children to play involves movement around the room, remove any obstacles and make sure that the play area is safe. For games that are played in two teams, the same teams can be kept throughout the school year so that no time is lost in choosing teams each time.

The preparation and setting up of a game presents a valuable opportunity for using classroom language. The instructions for the moving of desks and chairs, organisation into groups, preparation of materials, etc. may even be done in English in the early stages.

Before starting a game, it is essential that the children know what the language focus is, as the excitement generated during the game can obscure the linguistic objective. Demonstrate clearly how the game works and pre-teach the key language that the children will need. Write the key language on the board for children to refer to throughout the game.

Games played in small groups require effective monitoring. Make sure that each group is playing the game correctly, that English is the main language of communication for playing the game (though do not expect the children to use English exclusively) and that the children are not becoming overexcited or disruptive. This is also a good opportunity for the teacher to interact with the children in smaller groups and on an individual level in order to identify specific difficulties. You may feel it is not the right time to correct any student errors, as this may disrupt the game. It is a good idea to take note of the most common errors and focus on them after the activity.

Songs

A further source of language practice is provided by the songs and raps that appear in *Quest*. In many aspects of life children are keen to emulate older people and seek out role models. This is true of tastes in music and so the songs, chants and raps in *Quest* provide the kind of music and overall effect that children will identify as being 'adult' in terms of sound yet manageable in terms of language. The songs involve modern dance movement and they are fun to sing. Children love singing and the songs provide an effective and entertaining way of achieving natural stress and rhythm and giving additional pronunciation and intonation practice. Most of the units in *Quest* include a task-based song which not only consolidates the language of the unit but recycles previously learnt items and represents them in an extended context that the children will enjoy.

Hints on using songs

Before attempting to teach a song, let the children listen to it once or twice to get an idea of the rhythm. If the children are involved in a drawing, colouring or sticking activity, the songs may be played as background music. Once the children have heard the song a couple of times, you can get them to concentrate on the music following the rhythm to 'da da da' or 'la la la'. Then read the words a line at a time following the rhythm (rap style). Get the children to listen and repeat without the music. Explain the meaning of any passive language in the song. Once the children are familiar with the language content, put the words to the music a line or two at a time. Many of the songs are accompanied by actions or mimes, so teach the actions as part of the exploitation of the song. It is nice for the children to have an English music session singing the songs they have done one after another and the songs also provide good material for class shows.

Projects and surveys

Quest includes projects and surveys as part of the core material in the Student's Book and also as extra activities in the Teacher's Book.

The projects are of great cross-curricular value and help to practise target language in an extended context as well as drawing upon other skills, e.g. drawing, colouring, deciding on content, collecting things from outside the classroom and short writing tasks. The results of project work make attractive and useful classroom displays. The surveys involve the children in different ways of collecting and presenting data. They provide a range of patterns of interaction with the children often answering questions individually, then in groups and finally interpreting the data for the whole class. The extended nature of surveys provides ample practice of target language.

Culture Vulture pages

The *Culture Vulture* pages provide the children with a window onto everyday situations in countries where English is used.

The objective of the *Culture Vulture* pages is not only to present a realistic extension of the language covered in the unit but also to help the children discover that other children may have different lifestyles and routines. Although *Quest* 3 only contains three formal *Culture Vulture* sections, there is ample scope for teachers to develop various themes should they wish to pursue culture-based projects. Where there is the possibility of such an extension, this has been highlighted as a 'Teaching hint'.

The Teacher's Book

The *Quest* Teacher's Book contains step-by-step teaching notes for the core material in the Student's Book and suggestions for a wide range of extra activities. It aims to provide the teacher with a guide which is simple and enjoyable to use, yet at the same time, rewarding from a professional point of view. It has been written for experienced and less experienced teachers alike. One of its key features is flexibility which derives from an optional 'teaching path' which, while guiding some, does not slow down others or limit the creativity of either.

With the exception of Unit 2, which has five lessons, the material in each of the nine story units is dealt with over four lessons in the Teacher's Book. All the lessons contain natural break points where you may conveniently finish if time is short.

The main features of the Teacher's Book are as follows:

The 'teaching path'

The 'teaching path' is a visual representation of the stages of the lesson. The path runs down the left-hand side of the general teaching notes and allows the teacher to see at a glance the types of activities that are used and the patterns of interaction. Each activity and key stage is identified by an icon, some of which are the same as the ones contained in the Student's Book (see page 13).

The icons in the Teacher's Book

 indicates a listening activity which requires a cassette player and the correct tape

 indicates a *Story time* session

 indicates a presentation phase or a teacher-led phase

 indicates an activity that the children do in pairs

 indicates an activity that the children do in small groups or a mingling activity

 indicates a drama or roleplay activity

 indicates an *Escape door* activity

 indicates a drawing or writing activity

 indicates where resource material is needed

 indicates a 'Teaching hint' (see page 17)

Language focus box

Each lesson in the Teacher's Book has a summary of the key aspects of the lesson in the form of a language focus box. This contains the following information about the lesson – the objectives in functional terms, the target language, the language items which are recycled, the language items which are previewed, and the materials you will need. Glue, scissors and coloured pencils are not mentioned as it is assumed the children will have these items. Check the language focus box before each lesson to help you prepare for the lesson.

Recycled language

Presenting language in varying contexts and using known lexis to introduce structures (or vice versa) allows the child not only to broaden his/her experience of the language, but also to gradually achieve flexibility in the use of English. This enables the child to continually reorder his/her knowledge in order to adapt to new situations when communicating with others. For this reason the language introduced in *Quest* 1 and 2 is regularly integrated into the *Quest* 3 syllabus and highlighted in the language focus box at the beginning of each lesson.

Preview

The language items included in this section appear in the next episode of the story. The objective of using these items contextualised during class activities is to clarify the meaning and provide the children with a sense of familiarity when the items come up in the story episode.

Extra activities

The Teacher's Book contains a wide range of suggestions for extra activities which give further practice of the target language. They consist of games, project work, roleplay, etc. and they offer the teacher greater flexibility in the timing of the lesson and in providing extra support and consolidation.

Escape door activities

In the course of the notes in the Teacher's Book there are *Escape door* activities. These 'doors' allow the teacher to 'escape' from the book and widen the focus of subjects introduced by the target language. *Escape doors* may lead to drama, art-and-craft activities, class projects, etc. These activities are not strictly linked to the language exponents in the unit, but *Escape doors* offer the children the opportunity to explore areas of interest that derive from the topic as well as share knowledge from other areas of their studies.

The amount of time an *Escape door* activity lasts will vary. Some are relatively short and could round off a lesson, while others may require a full lesson in order to fully exploit the material.

'Teaching hint'

The teacher's notes contain a wide range of 'Teaching hints'. These are practical suggestions for class management which help the teacher get the most out of an activity as well as warn of any pitfalls that need to be avoided.

Photocopiable resource material

There is a photocopiable resource section at the back of the Teacher's Book, which consists of ready-to-use, time-saving material such as illustrative material, maps and material for games (see pages 121–160). The teacher's notes contain clear references to this material so that the teacher can prepare photocopies in advance.

INTRODUCTORY UNIT

Lesson 1

OBJECTIVES:	to re-establish contact with English
	to revise language from *Quest* 1 and 2
RECYCLED LANGUAGE:	language from *Quest* 1 and 2
MATERIALS:	photocopies of resource page 121

Introduction

The main objective of the Introductory Unit is to get the children thinking about English again and to revise the language learnt in *Quest* 1 and 2. The material for this unit is designed to cover two lessons and it appears only in the Teacher's Book.

1 Remind the children of the story in *Quest* 2, and in which civilisations the action took place (Atlantis, real world, Egyptian, Celtic, Roman), and ask them which part of the story they enjoyed most.

2 Get the children to mingle and to ask each other *What's your favourite unit/episode?* Then they make notes of their answers.

3 Tell the children that this information will be summarised in a bar chart showing the various civilisations (above) so that it will show the civilisation in which their favourite episodes took place, e.g. if one child likes Unit 5 best and another prefers Unit 6, both results will be shown in the Egyptian bar on the chart.

1 Talk about the picture.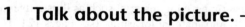

1 Hand out copies of resource page 121 and give the children sufficient time to observe the scene. It contains various visual stimuli aimed at eliciting much of the language learnt in *Quest* 2, namely, the weather, clothes, actions, nationalities, feelings and moods, date, time, homes and furniture.

2 Ask the children *Can you tell me something about this picture?* Encourage them to call out the names of objects they recognise, what people are doing, wearing, etc.

3 Help them by asking more specific questions like *Look at this boy. What's he doing/wearing? Has he got a hat? Is he happy? Is he wearing jeans? Is he eating? What's the time/date? What's the weather like? How many houses are there? Where's the van?* etc.

4 Model and drill *pub*.

2 True or False? ——————

1 Write the following statements on the board.

1 *The weather today is cold and windy.*	2 *There are a boy and a girl sitting near the pub.*
3 *The boy is eating chicken and chips.*	4 *The children are playing.*
5 *One of the children is tall.*	6 *In the picture there are a sofa, a wardrobe and an armchair.*
7 *There is a man from India.*	8 *It's the nineteenth of June.*
9 *It's a quarter past eleven.*	10 *There are six houses in the picture.*

2 Ask the children to look at the photocopy of the street scene and to decide whether these statements are true or false.

3 They check their answers in pairs.

Key

1 F 2 T 3 F 4 T 5 T 6 T 7 T 8 F 9 F 10 F

3 Who is Julia? Who is Max?

1 Tell the children that you are going to read the descriptions of Julia and Max, a girl and a man in the picture.

2 They have to listen carefully, and decide which girl is Julia and which man is Max.

Julia has got long dark hair. She's tall and thin. She's wearing a skirt and a jacket. She's listening to music.

Max is wearing shorts and a shirt. He's near the museum. He's got a cowboy hat. He's from America.

4 Write and check.

1 Ask the children to work individually. They have to number the characters on the photocopy and write five sentences about what they see in the street scene. The sentences they produce can be either true or false.

2 When they have finished writing their sentences, they pass them to a partner who has to read the sentences and say if they are true or false.

3 He/She then passes the sheet back to the first child, who checks the answers.

5 Look and colour.

Individually, the children observe the scene and colour in all the items that they feel they can say something about, e.g. *This is a house. He's eating (a sandwich)*, etc.

6 Write the sentences.

1 Identify an area of language you would like to revise (clothes, *there is/are, he's/she's got*, etc.) and write a series of prompts on the board for the children to copy and extend in order to practise that linguistic area.

2 For example, if you wish to practise the present continuous, you could write the following true and false prompts on the board:

1 *a boy/eat/sandwich*   2 *a girl/drink/Coke*   3 *a girl/look at/the street*
4 *Julia/listen to/music*   5 *a boy/wear/skates*   6 *a man/ride/a bike*

3 As an example, you could expand the first one: *A boy is eating a sandwich.*

Lesson 2

OBJECTIVES:	to re-establish contact with English
	to revise language from *Quest* 1 and 2
RECYCLED LANGUAGE:	language from *Quest* 1 and 2
MATERIALS:	card (approx. 50cm x 50cm), photocopies of resource page 121

7 Word grouping.

1 Write the words below all over the board, at random. If you prefer, write them on a sheet of paper to photocopy and hand out.

sunny, windy, cloudy, raining; jacket, coat, sunglasses, anorak; skateboard, bike, computer game,

19

INTRODUCTORY UNIT

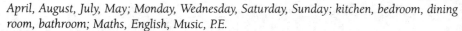

April, August, July, May; Monday, Wednesday, Saturday, Sunday; kitchen, bedroom, dining room, bathroom; Maths, English, Music, P.E.

2   Tell the children that these are all words they learnt last year and they have to put them into logical groups: clothes, weather, toys, months, days, rooms, subjects.

8   Picture labelling

1   The children stick the now coloured-in scene from the previous lesson on to a piece of card which is larger than the scene, so that they can write the following questions around it.
2   Ask the children to label the items in the scene with questions concerning each part of it, for example they can link *What's the weather like?* to the sun, or *What's the date?* to the date on the street scene, and so on.

What's the weather like?	*What's this?*	*Is it a sandwich?*
What's the date?	*What's he/she wearing?*	*Where are they?*
What's he/she doing?	*Has he/she got a walkman?*	*How many houses are there?*

9   Put the months in the correct order.

1   Remind the children of the date on the picture from Lesson 1 and ask them if they remember the other months of the year.
2   Write the months on the blackboard, at random. The children have to decide the correct order, and write them in their exercise books.

10   Write the dates.

1   Focus attention on the date in the street scene from Lesson 1 (19th) and ask the children why there is *th* after the number 19. Revise the ordinal numbers, paying particular attention to their pronunciation.
2   Write some ordinal numbers in full on the blackboard, ask the children to copy them in their exercise books and to write the abbreviated form of each ordinal number next to the corresponding number.

11   Special dates

1   As this is the start of the new school year, the children can make a list of their important dates for the coming year, too. These dates can be birthdays, start of the holidays, back to school, festivities, school trips, shows, etc. Tell the children that they are going to make a wall chart to remember the dates.
2   First revise the months and the ordinal numbers. Ask some children *When's your birthday?*
3   Prepare the wall chart containing the twelve months of the year (in three columns of four rows), leaving a space at least 15 centimetres wide and about 8–10 centimetres deep, to allow for three or four strips from resource page 122 to be stuck in under each month. The children could decorate each month with some indication of the season.
4   With the children, decide on what the important dates are, and write them on the board.
5   Hand out copies of resource page 122, and ask the children what they think each small picture on the strips represents. (birthdays, trips, etc.) Explain that they are going to complete these and put them in position on the wall chart.
6   Write model sentences on the board, e.g. *Marco's birthday is on the 22nd. Christmas holidays begin/finish on the (23rd). The school trip to ... is on the ... . There's a show on the ...,* etc. and assign these to various children who copy the sentences on to the appropriate strip.
7   Stick the various events on to the wall chart in the appropriate place and order. During the school year the chart can be updated if planned activities change.

SPACE ATTACK!

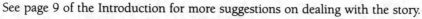

Story time

See page 9 of the Introduction for more suggestions on dealing with the story.

1 In L1, tell the children that in *Quest* 3 they are going to read and listen to a story. Get them to look at the pictures in the first few episodes. Elicit a few details about the characters and the places and get the children to predict the type of story they are going to read.

2 Focus attention on the title *Space Attack!*, and in L1 explain what this means. Let the children observe the pictures in Episode 1 for a while and then ask them where they think this scene is set (*our solar system*). Ask them if they know the names of any other planets and if they know these names in English.

3 Use the scenes to recycle language that the children have already covered: *Look at the boy! What colour are his eyes? Is he tall? How old is he? Look! This is his mother. She's got a crown. She's a queen. How many guards? How many spaceships?* Focus attention on the other characters and elicit *guard*. For each character, ask *Is he good/nasty/tall/short/fat/thin/nice/ beautiful*, etc.

4 Tell the children that they are going to hear the first episode of the story and that you want them to follow the action by putting their fingers on the appropriate picture as they listen. Tell them not to focus on individual words but to try and follow the episode in general. Play the recording of the episode through once. Check the children have understood by getting them to summarise briefly the episode in L1.

5 Play the tape again and get the children to put their hands up each time they find out the name of one of the characters (*Kanda, Rui, Marla, Damek Za*). Pause the tape as the children put their hands up and check.

6 Play the tape once again and get the children to listen and find out:
  a where the aliens are from (*Arion*).
  b who Damek Za is (*Rui's brother*).
  c why Damek Za attacks them (*He wants to be the new king of Arion*).
  Invite the children to call out all language items they already know in the episode.

7 Get the children to look at the episode again and make sure they have understood that:
  a Kanda, Marla and Rui are aliens on a journey through space.
  b they are entering Earth's solar system.
  c they are attacked.
  d Marla and Rui manage to help Kanda escape to Earth in a space capsule.
  e before leaving, Damek Za damages their engines and computer to stop them returning to Arion.
  f Marla and Rui try to contact Earth for help.

Lesson 1

OBJECTIVES:	to identify the names of the planets in our solar system; to identify planets by simple descriptions
TARGET LANGUAGE:	planets (*Mercury, Venus, Earth, Mars, Jupiter, Saturn, Uranus, Neptune, Pluto*), moon, planet, rings, solar system, space, spaceship, spot, star, sun
RECYCLED LANGUAGE:	adjectives, colours, ordinal numbers, *it is/it's got*, features of the countryside
PREVIEW:	*It's very nice!*
MATERIALS:	cassette player, cassette 1, photocopies of resource page 123

SPACE ATTACK!

Introduction

Using the storyline pages, revise numbers by asking the children simple questions like *How many pictures are there? (fourteen) How many people are there on Rui's/Damek Za's spaceship?* Point to each picture in turn and say *This is the first picture. This is the second ... .* Encourage the children to carry on the count.

1 Listen and point. Listen and repeat.

See page 13 of the Introduction for more suggestions on dealing with the *Listen and repeat* activities.

1 Focus attention on the picture showing the solar system. Explain that the captain of a spaceship is describing our solar system to his crew. Ask the children if they can imagine what he is saying, e.g. *This is Mars!/It's nice/Look here!/There are nine planets,* etc.

2 Ask the class if they remember the names of any of the planets mentioned in the story. Point out where the sun is and explain that they are going to learn the names of all the planets, from left to right.

3 Mime and say *Repeat!* Play the tape and get the children to repeat. Model and drill the sentences.

Tapescript

Man   This is the solar system. There are nine planets. The first planet is Mercury. The second is Venus. The third is Earth. The fourth is Mars. The fifth is Jupiter. The sixth is Saturn. The seventh is Uranus. The eighth is Neptune. The ninth is Pluto.

4 Hold up the page of the book, or better, do a quick copy of the diagram on the blackboard. Point to various planets and ask, e.g.
   T   *Is this Jupiter?*   C   *No, it's Saturn.*
   T   *Which planet is this?*   C   *It's Pluto.*

5 Include the ordinal numbers and colours in the simple descriptions asking, e.g.
   T   *Which planet is Mercury?*   C   *It's the first planet.*
   T   *What colour is it?*   C   *It's light brown.*
   T   *Look at Saturn! It's got rings.* (Mime *rings*.) *Has (Earth) got rings?*   C   *No!*

6 Play a guessing game with the class. Say, e.g. *This is the fourth planet, it's red!* Let the children call out the name.

7 In pairs, child A points to a planet and child B describes it. Encourage the children to say the colours too, e.g. *This is (Pluto). It's the ninth planet in the solar system. It's grey and blue.*

2 Read and write.

Focus attention on the five fact cards and explain that each card describes one of the planets in the solar system, and that the names of the planets are written around the cards so that they can copy the correct spelling. They read the cards and write in the name of the planet.

Key
1 Pluto   2 Earth   3 Saturn   4 Mercury   5 Jupiter

3 SONG: Kanda

See page 15 of the Introduction for more suggestions on dealing with songs and raps.

1 Hand out photocopies of the resource material on page 123. Focus attention on the drawing and ask the children what they see. Point out the rubric below the text *Listen and*

find the missing planet. Ask them how they think the activity works. (In the song all but one of the planets are named.)

2 Tell them they are going to listen to the song. Play the tape and ask the children to point to the planets as they are mentioned.

3 Play the tape again and encourage the children to tick the planets when mentioned so that the missing one is clear (*Uranus*).

4 Let the children listen to the song a few times, getting them to join in first with the chorus and then with the verse as well.

Extension: feelings

Ask the children if the song transmits happiness, sadness, calm, anxiety, etc. Ask them which moment in the story the song reflects and who could be singing it (*Marla and Rui* – they are worried about what has happened to Kanda down on Earth).

Escape door: make a solar system mobile

Using polystyrene balls of different sizes if available, and if not, card discs cut out and coloured, the children can make a solar system mobile. They will also need two wire clothes hangers, one inside the other to form a cross, and some light nylon string. When the mobile is ready, mime and say *It's very nice!*

As a more ambitious project, the classroom could be used to house the mobile, and the exact proportions of the planets calculated with the mathematics teacher. A line can be hung across the room, the sun placed in one corner and the planets arranged in the appropriate order across the room.

Lesson 2

OBJECTIVES:	to compare physical features
TARGET LANGUAGE:	comparatives and superlatives (*Earth is bigger than Pluto. / Pluto is the smallest planet*), far
RECYCLED LANGUAGE:	adjectives, planets, animals
MATERIALS:	cassette player, cassette 1

4 Listen and repeat.

See page 13 of the Introduction for more suggestions on dealing with the *Listen and repeat* activities.

1 Focus attention on the picture and ask the children what they think the differences are between the two planets shown. Ask them what the thermometers and the two lines represent (temperature and relative size).

2 Explain that the man and the woman in the picture are studying our solar system and they are examining the differences between Earth and Pluto. Highlight the fact that this is a comparison by using mime.

3 Play the tape and encourage the children to repeat.

SPACE ATTACK!

4   To illustrate the comparative form, draw a large planet on the blackboard and say *This planet is big!* Draw an even bigger one and say *This planet is bigger than this one!*

5   Draw a hippo and say *This animal is big!* Say *Can you draw a bigger animal?* If the children draw an elephant, confirm it by saying *Yes, good! An elephant is bigger than a hippo.*

6   Use the same procedure with *colder.* Start with a well-known cold place in their country and then compare it with the North Pole.

5   Look and colour. Listen and link.

1   Revise the adjectives by asking the children *What's the opposite of cold/big/hot/small?*

2   Mime *near* with your hands and ask *Do you remember what this means?* Tell them that the opposite of *near* is *far* and drill the new word using choral drilling.

3   Focus attention on the drawing in Activity 4. Help the class to understand the mechanism *big/bigger, cold/colder,* pointing to a big/cold planet and to a bigger/colder one.

4   Focus the attention on the written form. Tell the children they're going to listen to other examples, but, before that, they can guess what will go with *small.*

5   After that, ask them to colour each of the adjectives on the left in a different colour. (You can give them suggestions on how to do this, e.g. 'hot' colours for *big, hot,* and *near* and 'cold' colours for *small, cold* and *far;* or the children can choose their own colours.) They then use the same colours for the corresponding comparative form on the right.

6   Play the tape. The children listen and point to the correct adjective.

7   Play the tape again and ask the children to link the adjectives by following the colour code they have established.

Tapescript

big ... bigger	hot ... hotter	near ... nearer
cold ... colder	far ... farther	small ... smaller

8   Point to the various planets and ask the children if they recognise them.

9   Point to Jupiter and, following the line in the example, say *Jupiter is bigger than Saturn.*

10 Elicit the next comparison saying *Venus is hot. Venus is hotter than ... .* Encourage the children to finish the sentence. (The name of any planet colder than Venus is acceptable.)

11 Tell them they are going to listen to the tape three times. The first time they point to the planets and comparatives mentioned, the second time they check that they have linked the adjectives and the comparative forms correctly. The third time they listen and repeat.

Tapescript

Now listen and check. Listen and repeat.

Jupiter is bigger than Saturn.	Venus is hotter than Earth.
Mercury is smaller than Neptune.	Pluto is colder than Uranus.
Saturn is farther than Earth.	Mars is nearer than Neptune.

6   Look and describe.

1   In pairs, child A looks at the planets and produces sentences following the model given in Activities 4 and 5.

2   Child B has to check whether the sentences produced are true/false, right/wrong, e.g. *Mercury is bigger than Pluto.* (T), *Saturn is hotter than Venus.* (F).

Extension: classroom objects

Show the class a classroom object and ask them questions like *What's this? Whose is it? What colour is it? Is it big or small?*, etc. to elicit the name, the colour, the size of the object, e.g. *It's Simon's rubber. It's red and blue. It's big.*

Do the same with another rubber and then show the two rubbers together to elicit the comparative form.

Repeat the activity by pointing to a child's desk and ask *What's this? (It's a desk.) Whose is it? (It's Jenny's desk.) Is it near the blackboard? (No, it isn't.) Which desk is nearer than Jenny's desk? (This/Gemma's desk is nearer.)*

7 Listen and repeat.

See page 13 of the Introduction for more suggestions on dealing with the *Listen and repeat* activities.

1 Compare three rubbers, of different colours, in terms of size. Point to each in turn saying, e.g. *The blue rubber is bigger than the green rubber. The green rubber is bigger than the red rubber. The blue rubber is the biggest.*

2 In order to highlight the meaning of *the biggest* repeat the same example with mime, pausing for effect when you indicate and describe the biggest rubber.

3 To clarify the meaning of the superlative, repeat the activity with other classroom objects, e.g. pencil sharpeners.

4 Ask the children to look at the picture and elicit why they think the planets are in this order (order of size).

5 Play the tape and ask the children to repeat. Model and drill the two sentences.

8 Complete the sentences.

1 This is a game of deduction. The children have to write in the name of the planet which corresponds to the description.

2 Point out that for sentences 2 and 3 there are more than one description and that the chosen planet must correspond to all the criteria.

Key

1 Jupiter   2 Mercury   3 Pluto

3 Using the children themselves illustrate and then practise the construction of superlative phrases, e.g. *John is the biggest.*

4 Ask the children *How many desks are near the blackboard?* and then *Which/Who is the nearest? (Debbie's desk/Debbie is the nearest (to the blackboard/door).*

5 Using the radiator/window you could practise *cold/hot* in the same way with *Which place is the hottest/coldest?*

9 Read and name.

1 Let the children observe the four spaceships. Explain that they have all been used for missions into space. Tell them to point to the biggest/smallest spaceship. Ask the class *Is this* (point to a spaceship) *bigger or smaller than* (point to another) *this one?*

2 Focus attention on the sentences and read out the first one, *Vostok is the smallest.* Tell the children to look at the pictures and point to the spaceship they think is Vostok.

3 The children write the name *Vostok* in the space provided, then individually they read the statements and name the remaining three spaceships.

SPACE ATTACK!

10 Now you try!

1 In pairs the children choose four planets and write sentences similar to those in Activity 9.
2 They hand their sheet of paper on to another pair of children, who have to guess the correct answers.

Lesson 3

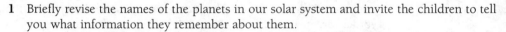

OBJECTIVES:	to develop reading comprehension skills; to discover information about the Earth and other places in the solar system
TARGET LANGUAGE:	extension of the superlative (*fattest, tallest, heaviest, longest*), measurements (*centimetre, metre, degree, kilogram, tonne*), *volcano, ocean, twin, whale*
RECYCLED LANGUAGE:	*there is/are, mountain, sea, woman*
PREVIEW:	*town*
MATERIALS:	cassette player, cassette 1

Introduction

1 Briefly revise the names of the planets in our solar system and invite the children to tell you what information they remember about them.
2 Encourage them by asking questions like *Which is the smallest/ biggest planet? Which planet is red/brown/green and blue? Which is the coldest/hottest planet?*
3 Tell the children they are going to learn some interesting facts about space, our solar system and the Earth.

11 Read and answer.

1 Focus attention on the first picture on page 9 and say *This is Io. It's one of Jupiter's moons. Jupiter has got sixteen moons.*
2 Indicate one of the volcanoes and say *This is a volcano!*
3 Go through the information on the page orally before getting the children to tackle the reading comprehension. This will give you the opportunity to stimulate interest and clarify and pre-teach any new lexis necessary for the activity, e.g. *high*.
4 As a class activity or individually/in pairs the children read, answer the questions, and then check with the rest of the class.

Key

The biggest volcano on Earth is Mauna Loa, Hawaii.
The highest mountain on Earth is Mount Everest.
There are four oceans: the Atlantic, the Arctic, the Indian and the Pacific. The biggest is the Pacific. The smallest is the Arctic.

Escape door: to represent planets

As a cross-curricular activity, examine with the children the relative proportionate sizes of planets related to everyday objects. This will help the children to imagine the actual size of each planet, e.g. Jupiter could be represented by a football, Earth by a marble. Find other common objects to represent the various planets considering their proportion.

12 Facts about the Earth. Listen and choose.

1 Ask the children if they have ever heard of *The Guinness Book of Records*. What kind of book is it? What information is in this book? Do they know any strange/interesting facts from this book?
2 Focus attention on the photos and tell the children they are taken from *The Guinness Book of Records*. Ask them why these people are in the book.
3 Read the information with the class and ask the children to try and guess the answers without giving any indication as to the correct answers at this stage.
4 Tell the children they are going to listen to the tape and get the answers.

Tapescript

This is Benny. He's the fattest twin brother on Earth! He's three hundred and forty-nine kilograms!

And this is Sandy. She's the tallest woman on Earth. Do you want to know how tall she is? Well, she's two metres and thirty-five centimetres tall.

Many animals are heavy, but the heaviest animals on Earth are whales. They can weigh as much as one hundred and ninety tonnes!

If you like hot places, why not visit Azizia? It's a town in Libya and is the hottest place on Earth. The record temperature was 58 degrees. Phew!

In space, the longest journey was made by Valeriy Poliyakov, who stayed in space for four hundred and thirty-seven days.

Key

1 349 Kg   2 2.35m   3 whales   4 Libya   5 437 days

Lesson 4

OBJECTIVES:	to talk about life in space; to express reasons and desire to do something; to develop reading skills
TARGET LANGUAGE:	*want* + infinitive
RECYCLED LANGUAGE:	present continuous, *can/can't, there is/isn't*
PREVIEW:	*Go over there!*
MATERIALS:	cassette player, cassette 1, photocopies of resource page 124

Introduction

Using the story as a focus point and reminding the children about Kanda and his mother and father on the Arion spaceship, talk about a 'space home' and what problems there might be (gravity, etc.).

13 Look, listen and number.

1 Focus attention on the illustration. First, ask questions about the picture, such as *What's this? (It's a spaceship.) How many people can you see? What's he/she doing? (cycling, watching TV, reading, eating, looking,* etc.) Ask about where things are, descriptions, activities, size, position, colours, clothes. (*What's he wearing? Where are they going?*)
2 Hand out copies of resource page 124. Tell the children they are going to listen to the tape

SPACE ATTACK!

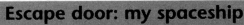

and answer the questions on the text by writing the number in the space provided.

3 Play the tape and ask the children to follow the description of the spaceship on the photocopy without trying to answer the questions.

4 Play the tape again and ask them to answer the questions. Stop the tape after each question to give them time to write.

5 Ask the children to read the text and decide if they are happy with the answers, then they check the answers in pairs.

6 Check the answers with the whole class.

Key
1 bed   2 toilet   3 shower   4 gym   5 computer/TV
6 drinking   7 shoes   8 telephone   9 kitchen   10 window

Escape door: my spaceship

Have the children draw their own imaginary spaceships and then describe them to each other. Elicit useful expressions and write them on the board. e.g. *This is my spaceship. There's a kitchen. On my spaceship I can ... . The ... is (between) the ... and the ... , etc.*

14 Listen and repeat.

See page 13 of the Introduction for more suggestions on dealing with the *Listen and repeat* activities.

1 Ask the children if they would like to travel in space. In L1 ask them where they would like to go and what they would like to see there.

2 Bring the theme round to travel on Earth. Again ask where they would like to go and what they would like to see.

3 Tell them they are going to listen to two children discussing this subject. Play the tape and ask them to repeat the questions and answers they hear.

4 When drilling the target structure, give the children a set rhythm to follow so that the long sentence is easier to produce. If necessary, break the sentence up and get the children to drill in three teams, e.g.
   A *Where do you want to go?*
   B *I want to go to Jupiter ...*
   C *... to see Jupiter's moons.*
Swap over and then split them into four groups.
   A *Where do you want to go?*
   B *I want to go to Jupiter ...*
   C *... to see Jupiter's moons.*
   D *I want to go to Jupiter to see Jupiter's moons!*
Let the teams take turns at each component.

5 Use the same procedure to practise *Where do you want to go? I want to go to Kenya to see the animals.*

15 Listen and match.

1 Tell them that they are going to listen to some children saying where they want to go and why.

2 The children listen to the tape and match the city or country to the appropriate photo by writing a number in the box.

Tapescript

Where do you want to go? I want to go to London to see the Queen.
Where do you want to go? I want to go to New York to see the Statue of Liberty.
Where do you want to go? I want to go to France to see Disneyland Paris.
Where do you want to go? I want to go to Australia to see the kangaroos.
Where do you want to go? I want to go to Rome to see the Colosseum.

3 In pairs, Child A asks *Where do you want to go?* Child B chooses a destination and answers, e.g. *I want to go to London to see the Queen.*
4 Encourage the children to offer their own personal ideas of where they want to go and what they want to see. Help them by supplying necessary vocabulary. Allow the children to use places in their own country as the objective here is to focus on the structure.

16 Now imagine ...

1 Tell the class that they can imagine they can go anywhere they like, either in space or on Earth. In order to go on this imaginary journey they have to plan it.

> **LANGUAGE FOCUS: only the travel card has been included in the Student's Book, since the primary focus of this activity is the flight of fancy for the children. The following language focus activity is a way of exploiting the structural aspects should you so wish. If not, the children simply complete the travel card and answer the teacher's questions orally.**

2 The children look at the log book and imagine what the questions are. For the first three they should have no difficulty in producing the right question.
3 Elicit from the children as much of the question as they are able to produce, helping them to formulate the whole question before presenting them with the written form.
4 Give out the questions photocopied on a sheet of paper (alternatively, the children could copy them from the board).

1 *What's your name?*	6 *How do you want to get there?*
2 *How old are you?*	7 *How many friends are with you?*
3 *Where do you want to go?*	8 *What are their names?*
4 *Why?*	9 *What do you want to take ?*
5 *When do you want to go?*	10 *What clothes do you want to take?*

5 Call out three children to read the first three questions, then ask the class to look at the remaining questions and underline each known word.
6 Model and drill the remaining questions.
7 Get the children into pairs and tell them they are going to do a role-play. One of them is the travel/space travel agency and the other is the passenger. Set up the situation and practise the questions again before they begin.

> **LIMITING SUGGESTIONS: to avoid neverending lists, for question 7 suggest a maximum of three friends; for question 9 let them choose anything they like or they think useful, but a maximum of three, e.g. their dog, their football team flag, their lucky charms.**

8 The children fill in the chart with their own answers.
9 Check the activity by asking a few questions to some children.

Drama time

1 Space Attack! (See page 10 of the Introduction for notes on *Drama time* for the story.)

2 NEW YORK

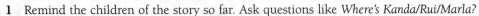

Story time

See page 9 of the Introduction for more suggestions on dealing with the story.

1 Remind the children of the story so far. Ask questions like *Where's Kanda/Rui/Marla?*
2 Get them to look at the pictures in the second episode. Focus attention on the title, and ask the children where they think this episode is taking place. Ask them if they recognise any of the characters on the first page. Ask *Who's this?* or *Who are they?* The children should have understood that Doctor Alpha, Ben and his friends have just arrived in New York. At this point, in L1, explain that they are visiting Ben's uncle who lives in New York, and he has invited them for a holiday. Ben's uncle is a very famous astrophysicist. He is always busy. He promised to be at the airport to meet them but he has had to go away on business unexpectedly. Ask the children what they would do if they were in Ben's place, and focus their attention on the last picture of the first page. Ask the children *What's he doing?* (*He's looking at a map.*) Let the children study the rest of the pictures in Episode 2 for a while and then encourage them to describe briefly what is happening in each scene. Make sure that the children have understood that:
   a Doctor Alpha, Jasper, Ben and his friends have just arrived at the airport in New York.
   b Doctor Alpha goes to the information desk because there's a message.
   c Uncle Otto cannot meet them at the airport because he is still in San Francisco.
   d they decide to go to the house by bus and during the journey they see various places.
   e when they get off the bus they ask directions to the house.
   f they arrive at the house, and the children go upstairs to look round while Doctor Alpha relaxes in the sitting room/laboratory.
   g the equipment is suddenly activated and Doctor Alpha gets up to see what is happening.
   h when the children come down into the room, they are astonished to see Doctor Alpha caught up in a beam of light.
3 Tell the children they are going to listen to the second episode of the story. Follow the *Story time* procedure on page 9 of the Introduction. Play the recording of the episode through once. The children should listen for the name of Ben's uncle (*Otto*).
4 Play the tape again and ask the children to discover:
   a where Uncle Otto is (*San Francisco*).
   b the name of the street they are looking for (*Roosevelt Street*).
   c the number of the house (*41*).
5 Write the following statements on the board and tell the children they are to decide whether they are true or false, as they listen to the tape again.
   1 The key is next to the mat. (F)
   2 There's a park opposite the house. (T)
   3 The children go upstairs to see the bathroom. (F)
   4 Ben says *Where's your nose, Dad?* (F)

Lesson 1

OBJECTIVES:	to ask about, suggest and choose means of transport
TARGET LANGUAGE:	suggestions (*Let's go by bus*), means of transport (*bus, train, ship, plane, motorbike, camper, underground, on foot*), *How do you get to ...?*
RECYCLED LANGUAGE:	*Let's ...,* bike, car
MATERIALS:	cassette player, cassette 1, photocopies of resource page 125

Introduction

1 Ask the children how they come to school in the morning and discuss their answers.
2 Remind them of the point in the story when Ben and the others arrived in New York and had to get to Otto's house. Ask them what method of transport they used (*bus*).

1 Listen and point. Listen and repeat.

See page 13 of the Introduction for more information on the *Listen and repeat* activities.

1 Focus attention on the various modes of transport, and elicit the names of those the children are already familiar with (*bus, bike, car*).
2 In L1, explain to them that they are going to learn the names of other means of transport. Tell them to listen to the tape and point to the correct means of transport. Play the tape.

Tapescript

Doctor Alpha   Let's go by bus. Let's go by train. Let's go by ship. Let's go by bike. Let's go by plane. Let's go by motorbike. Let's go by car. Let's go by camper. Let's go by underground. Let's go on foot.

3 Mime and say *Repeat!* Play the tape again and get the children to repeat. Drill the sentences using choral and group drilling.
4 Practise the new vocabulary by inviting the children to suggest ways of getting to a town or city they know. Then ask the children to continue in pairs:
A *Let's go to* (name of town/city)!   B *Let's go by* (train)!

2 Listen and guess.

1 Invite the children to make the noises produced by each of the various forms of transport.
2 Tell them they are going to listen to similar noises on the tape and they have to guess which they are. The children listen to the noises (including the footsteps) and guess by saying e.g. *by/on ... car/bus/bike/camper/plane/ship/train/underground/foot.*
3 When one of the noises is particularly easy, e.g. footsteps, say *That's easy!*

Tapescript and Key

1 car 2 bus 3 plane 4 train 5 camper 6 ship 7 bike 8 foot 9 motorbike 10 underground

3 Listen and choose.

1 Draw a car on the board. Elicit from the children words to describe the car/parts of the car (*doors, wheels*) and label the drawing and help the children to produce *It's a car. It's big. It's got four wheels/doors. It's smaller than a camper*, etc.
2 Focus attention on the drawings and elicit the means of transport illustrated.
3 Tell the children they are going to listen to four descriptions, each one describing one of these methods of transport. They have to tick the boxes of the ones being described.

Tapescript

1 If you're in London, it's red and very big. It's got ten wheels. You can sit downstairs or upstairs. It's got a number on the front. What is it?
2 It's got four wheels. It's smaller than a bus. It's got two or four doors. My Dad's has got four doors and it's a Fiat.
3 It's very long. You need a ticket. It travels under the city in tunnels.
4 It's got four wheels and it's bigger than a car. You can sleep in this, and there's a kitchen, a bathroom and beds.

NEW YORK

Key
1 bus 2 car 3 underground 4 camper

4 Ask and answer.

1 Ask the children if they have been to a major city in their country and how they got there. Discuss alternative ways.
2 Remind the children of the moment in the story when Doctor Alpha didn't know how to get to Otto's house. Encourage the children to remember what question he asked (*How do you get to ... ?*) and highlight this question as a means to ask for directions.
3 Practise the dialogue with the children by asking them how to get to towns or cities in their country.
4 Point out that there is often more than one way to get from one place to another, and focus the children's attention on the dialogue in the Student's Book, page 16, Activity 4.
5 Hand out copies of resource page 125 and give the children time to study it. Say *Look, this is Great Britain, and this is France*. Point to the various transport symbols and ask *What's this?*
6 Ask the children to practise the model dialogue by using the information on the map, e.g.
 A *We're in London. How do you get to Oxford?*
 B *By car or by train.*
 A *Let's go by car.*

Lesson 2

OBJECTIVES:	to identify places in town; to ask for and give information about where places in town are
TARGET LANGUAGE:	places in town (*hospital, sports centre, park, museum, swimming pool, amusement arcade, police station, cinema; post office, bank*)
RECYCLED LANGUAGE:	prepositions of place (*near, in, next to, opposite, between*), *library, school, What ... ? / Where ...? What's this? Is it ... ?*
PREVIEW:	short answer forms, *It's over there.*
MATERIALS:	cassette player, cassette 1, photocopies of resource page 126

Introduction

Remind them what Ben pointed to during the bus ride (*amusement arcade, sports centre*).

5 Listen and repeat. Read and match.

See page 13 of the Introduction for more information on the *Listen and repeat* activities.

1 Focus attention on the map and the numbered places. Ask the children if they recognise any of them. Tell them they are going to listen to the names as the bus moves along. Play the tape.

Tapescript

Doctor Alpha	The bus stop is over there.
Susan	Look! A police station.
Ben	a hospital
Toby	a museum
Susan	a cinema
Ben	a park
Toby	a swimming pool
Susan	a school
Ben	a sports centre
Toby	an amusement arcade

2 Mime and say *Repeat!* Play the tape again and get the children to repeat. Drill the sentences using choral and group drilling.

3 After they have listened and repeated, they number the appropriate words below the map.

6 Ask and answer.

1 Hand out copies of resource page 126. The children cut out the cards and colour them. They can draw places of their own choice in the three empty cards. Present, model and drill the new items *bank*, *cinema* and *post office* and the recycled item *library*.

2 In pairs the children ask and answer *What's this? It's a hospital* and/or *Is it a school? Yes, it is./No, it isn't.*

3 The children stick one set of cards around the classroom on the walls. They go around and ask their classmates *Excuse me, where's the hospital/cinema*, etc. At this stage the other child simply points to the appropriate card and answers *It's over there!*

DURABLE CARDS: to identify and differentiate this set of cards from other sets which will be used in future lessons, decide on a colour or design or a border to add to the back of each of these cards and have the children colour/draw it. Later sets can each have a different colour or design. This will make collecting and storing classroom sets of cards much easier. Once this identification has been added, it would make the cards more durable if they were backed with adhesive transparent paper.

Escape door: road signs

If the area in which the children live is a tourist area, this might be a good time to discuss the various symbols used on road signs, in brochures and in advertising material to help foreign visitors find the various services, sports facilities and amenities.

7 Draw, ask and answer.

1 Using the places dealt with in the previous activity, ask the children about the relative location of these places in their town. You could draw the main streets on the board if appropriate, and mark the positions. Ask *Where's the (bank)? Where's the (school)?* etc. Let the children refer to your drawing and say, e.g. *The (bank) is (near) the (post office).* Use this to revise prepositions *next to, opposite, near, between.*

2 Focus attention on the simple street plan and the two sets of four symbols. Ask the children *What's this?* (Group 1 *hospital, park, police station, cinema;* Group 2 *bank, post office, swimming pool, sports centre*).

3 Before starting the activity, model it on the board with a child. Look at the plan together and decide where to locate one of the eight places using the following dialogue:

A *Where's the (hospital)?*

B *It's opposite the museum.*

Draw the hospital (or write the word) in the appropriate place on the plan.

4 In pairs, the children look at the plan together and have a similar conversation to locate the eight (or the other seven) places. Then they draw the place on the map.

Lesson 3

OBJECTIVES:	to identify the points of the compass; to ask for/give information about where you live
TARGET LANGUAGE:	the points of the compass (*north, north-east, east, south-east, south, south-west, west, north-west*), *city, town, village, Where do you live?*
RECYCLED LANGUAGE:	prepositions of place (*in, near, next to, opposite, between*), places in town and the environment, *What ... ? / Where ...? / Is there? / Is it ... ?*, short answer forms, comparatives and superlatives
PREVIEW:	*I think it's ... . You're right!*
MATERIALS:	cassette player, cassette 1, photocopies of resource pages 127–128

8 Listen and repeat. Read and match.

See page 13 of the Introduction for more information on the *Listen and repeat* activities.

1 Focus attention on the points of the compass. Ask the children where they might see this and what its function is. Ask who needs it and when it would be used.

2 Explain that the cardinal points are shown in the diagram. Ask if they recognise the letters and what they stand for. Tell them they are going to listen to these words in English. The children listen and follow the points round the diagram and then listen and repeat.

Tapescript

north   north-east   east   south-east   south   south-west   west   north-west

3 Use the classroom to ask the children where the various points are, e.g. *Where's north?* Stand in the middle of the classroom, call one child and place him/her in the position 'north'. Say *That's north!* Call out another child and say *You're in the north-east.* The child should stand in the correct place. Continue with the other cardinal points. If the child stands in the correct place, mime and say *You're right!* If not, correct him/her gently by miming and saying *Hmmm, I think it's (there)!*

4 Finally, ask them to read and match the cardinal points to the points of the compass.

9 Listen and read. Read and mark F, or T or ?

1 Focus attention on the three drawings on the right-hand side of the page. Ask the children how they would describe these 'settlements' in their own language. Tell them they are going to listen to the names in English and then answer some simple questions.

Tapescript

Look at numbers one, two and three.

Number one is a city, number two is a town, number three is a village.

A city is very big. It's bigger than a town. A town is smaller than a city, but bigger than a village. A village is very small.

Listen and answer.

Which is the biggest? Which is the smallest? Do you live in a village, a town or a city?

2 Encourage the children to answer, and ask them for examples of towns, cities and villages in their country.

3 Tell the children they are going to listen to a girl, Frankie, talking about where she lives. Explain that they should follow what she is saying in their books.

> **LISTENING AND READING: as they are listening, stop the tape before a familiar word and get the children to call out which word is coming. This will ensure that the children are following accurately at the speed of the taped information.**

4 Play the tape again and then give them a short time to read through the text again at their own speed.

5 Focus attention on the sentences and read them through together, giving explanations where necessary. Explain that the sentences are linked to the text they have just read and that they have to indicate if they are true or false, or if the information is not given. The first has been answered as an example.

Key
1 F   2 T   3 F   4 ?   5 F   6 F   7 ?   8 F

10 Play and draw.

1 Hand out copies of resource pages 127–128 and let the children colour them.

2 Put all 32 cards (including the blank cards, which are to be used for anything else the children choose) on the board and let the children look at them and identify what each card shows.

3 Explain that they must ask and answer questions relating to the cards and their idea of a good town to live in.

4 The activity is managed as a game, and the objective of the game is to build a place in which the children would like to live. Explain the rules of the game, which are:

   a the number of items in the place will depend on how big it is: if they decide to build a village they may include 7 items, a town needs 10, and a city 15.

   b based on the language chain on page 19 of the Student's Book, the game goes around the class with one child answering his/her classmate's question and then asking the next question him/herself.

   c when a child answers a question and receives an answer, he/she must go to the board and take the appropriate card.

   d the answers given gradually build up a description of the town/city/village.

5 Before starting the game, reserve an area of the board where the children can stick the cards they choose.

6 The first time you play the game, model it using the illustrations and the language chain.

NEW YORK

DUPLICATE CARDS: the children may well decide to put more than one of each item in their town, e.g. two parks. For this reason, it would be a good idea to photocopy these popular items and thus have more than one card available. Alternatively, they could write the number they want of each item next to the card on the board.

Extension: further use of the cards

The cards can also be used for other practice activities. For example, in pairs, have one child arrange the cards along an imaginary road and together they ask and answer questions, e.g.

A *Where's the school?* **B** *It's opposite the bank.*

or

A *It's next to the (school).* **B** *Umm ... It's the (bank)!*

As writing practice, put up a selection of cards on the board and explain that this is the town/village/city you have constructed. The children write a guided description starting *In this (town) there ...* and ending with a guided sentence, such as *I like this (town) because ... / ... I don't like this (town) because ...* .

11 PROJECT: Where do you live?

The children draw or collect material about their town (where they come to school) and make a wall chart with a description underneath following the model of Frankie's home town.

Lesson 4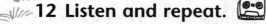

OBJECTIVES:	to be able to read a map; to ask for/give directions
TARGET LANGUAGE:	directions vocabulary (*Excuse me, where's ... ? / Turn left/right. / Go straight on. / Take the underground.*), *street, road, building*
RECYCLED LANGUAGE:	prepositions of place (*in, near, next to, opposite, between*), places in town, comparatives and superlatives, *Where's ... ?*
MATERIALS:	cassette player, cassette 1, photocopies of resource page 129

Introduction

Remind the children of how Doctor Alpha and the children got to Otto's house from the airport. Ask them how Doctor Alpha found out where the house was and what happened. Ask the children if anything similar has ever happened to them.

12 Listen and repeat.

See page 13 of the Introduction for more information on the *Listen and repeat* activities.

1 Focus attention on the presentation flash pointing out the gestures accompanying the directions and ask the children to identify the direction each person gives.

2 Tell the class they are going to learn how to ask for directions and how to direct someone who asks them. Play the tape.

3 Mime and say *Repeat!* Play the tape again and get the children to repeat. Drill the sentences using choral and group drilling.

4 Ask the children what question(s) you could ask a passer-by in a town you don't know. Give the children prompts, e.g. *London Street.* The children ask *Excuse me, where's London Street?*

5 Continue with other names of roads and streets. Use the names that will appear in Activity 14, so as to familiarise them with the names. Give them cues to recycle names associated with places in town, e.g. *Excuse me, where's the bank/park/bridge?*

6 Once you have modelled the question form, add the reply. Get the children to associate an arm movement with each of the three directions to elicit *Go straight on! Turn right! Turn left!*

13 GAME: Listen and move

See page 15 of the Introduction for more suggestions on dealing with games.

Using objects as 'mines', a blindfold child (or with eyes really closed!) has to follow instructions from his/her friends in order to avoid the 'mines' strewn around the floor. Recap on the instructions that could be useful during the game, e.g. *Go straight on! Turn right! Turn left!* and add *Stop!*

14 Listen and find. Read and find.

1 Focus attention on the map rather than what is written under it. The text on the page is the same as the tape.

2 Explain that the children will have to listen to instructions and follow them in order to discover their final destination.

3 Read out the names of the streets and roads on the map, and get the children to find them and point to them. Do the same with some of the places marked on the map.

4 Give the children a few minutes to study the map carefully.

5 Set up the activity and model it using the following two examples:
You're outside the hotel. Turn right into High Street and go straight on. Turn right into West Street. There's a building here, opposite the police station. What is it? (the museum)
You're outside the post office. Turn right and then turn left into Clayton Street. Go straight on, turn right. There's a building here. What is it? (the library)

ORIENTATION: point out that when you follow directions on a map, left and right will depend on which way you are facing!

6 Play the tape and ask the children to follow the routes on the map.

7 Play the tape again and ask them to trace the routes on the map.

8 Check that the routes they have drawn are correct. Tell them to read the text and complete it with the missing words. If you prefer, you can write the missing words on the board in a jumbled order to facilitate the task.

Key
1 Royal bridge left London opposite   2 Arcade right left

9 Now ask the children to answer the questions related to the two texts.

Key
1 a school   2 a park

NEW YORK

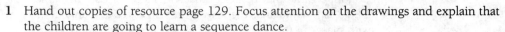

15 Ask and answer.

In pairs, the children choose a destination and ask e.g. *Where's the library?* The other child gives instructions to reach this place, e.g. *Go straight on!* etc.

16 SONG: The line rap

See page 15 of the Introduction for more suggestions on dealing with songs and raps.

1 Hand out copies of resource page 129. Focus attention on the drawings and explain that the children are going to learn a sequence dance.
2 You will need a line on the floor (chalk or imaginary). The children start behind the line, do the sequence – which involves a series of movements – and then return to their original starting position 'back behind the line'.
3 Before playing the rap, go through the words with the class to give them more confidence.
4 Go through the words again and get the children to repeat the words after you, gradually building up the rhythm.
5 Let them listen to the rap and join in with the words.
6 When they are confident, start getting them familiar with the movements to accompany the rap. A suggested routine is as follows:

Tapescript	*Suggested Movements*
One step forward	All take one step forward across the line
Face your partner	Each child turns left or right to face his/her partner
Clap your hands and	All clap hands against those of their partners
Back behind the line.	All go quickly back to the starting position
Go straight on – one	All take one step forward
Go straight on – two	All take another step forward
Hands together and	All join hands
Back behind the line.	All go quickly back to the starting position.
Chorus	
Rap it, clap it	All the children take one step forward
You can sing it or tap it	and stay there, making free
Rap it, clap it!	movements or dancing, clapping hands
Do what you want but	in rhythm
Back behind the line!	All go quickly back to the starting position.
Turn round quickly	Children turn 180°
Step back slowly	All take one step backwards (over the line)
Turn left, turn right	All turn to the left then to the right
Back behind the line.	All go quickly back to the starting position.
Go straight on – one	All take one step forward
Go straight on – two	All take another step forward
Hands together and	All join hands
Back behind the line.	All go quickly back to the starting position.

Lesson 5

OBJECTIVES: to find out about places in London
TARGET LANGUAGE: Science Museum, Buckingham Palace, Madame Tussaud's, Planetarium, London Zoo, Hamley's, Trocadero, Tower of London
RECYCLED LANGUAGE: *How do you get to …?, crown, jewels, queen*
MATERIALS: cassette player, cassette 1, photocopies of resource pages 130–131

CULTURE VULTURE: A visit to London

17 Listen and choose.

1 Let the children observe the photos. Do they recognise any of the places? (They should remember the Tower of London.)
2 Explain what each place is and ask if any of them have ever been anywhere similar. Explain that Trocadero is a very big amusement arcade with all the latest electronic games and rides.
3 Elicit key vocabulary about each place so that you can expose them to the language they will hear on the tape, e.g *Buckingham Palace. It's very big. There are a lot of rooms. Who lives here? (the Queen). What can you find in the Science Museum? (aeroplanes, ships, spaceships, etc.)*
4 Tell the children that they are going to hear a description of the places but the names are not mentioned. The children have to listen and try to guess which place is being described and which picture each description refers to.
5 Let the children listen to the tape twice. The first time they listen and focus attention on the pictures. The second time they write the number of the description in the appropriate box.

Tapescript

1 This is a very big palace. There are 600 rooms. Queen Elizabeth lives here. What is it?
2 If you like spaceships, aeroplanes and science, this is the best museum for you. What is it?
3 This is a castle near the river. The Queen's crown and jewels are here. What is it?
4 If you like videogames and amusement arcades, this is the perfect place for you in Piccadilly. Take a lot of money! What is it?
5 You can't go to Mars, Jupiter or Saturn, but you can see all the stars and planets of the solar system here. What is it?
6 This place is near a very big park and you can see tigers, pandas, lions and a lot of other animals here. What is it?
7 This is the biggest toy shop in England. There are six floors full of dolls, games, videos, cars and other wonderful toys. What is it?
8 Do you want to see famous people, film stars and pop stars like Michael Jackson? Go to this museum, and you can see them, but they can't move. What is it?

NEW YORK

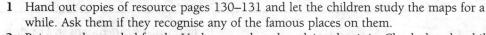

18 Listen and follow. Ask and answer.

1 Hand out copies of resource pages 130–131 and let the children study the maps for a while. Ask them if they recognise any of the famous places on them.

2 Point out the symbol for the Underground, and explain what it is. Check that the children understand which road/street they are in as they come out of the Underground station.

3 Ask the children what they would ask a policeman if they wanted to go to a place on one of the maps from the nearest Underground station. They will probably suggest *Excuse me, where's ...?* Accept this and then remind them of what Doctor Alpha asked the clerk at the airport (*How do you get to ...?*)

4 Point out the various places on the maps and ask them to tell you what they think they can see in each place. Here is a list of possible things they might like to see in each place:
Tower of London: crown jewels
Planetarium: solar system, stars, planets
Madame Tussaud's: wax models of famous people
Buckingham Palace: the Queen, royal guards (Household Cavalry, Grenadier Guards)
Houses of Parliament: Big Ben
Trafalgar Square: Nelson's Column
Science Museum: spaceships, (aero)planes, old cars
Natural History Museum: dinosaurs
Geological Museum: minerals, gemstones
Victoria & Albert Museum: old costumes
Write the names of the places on the board and next to each the name of one of the things they could see there.

5 Tell the children to imagine they are in London and they are talking to a friend about what to go and see. They then ask directions starting from an Underground station, so the first instruction will be *Take the Underground to ...* (the nearest station to their destination).

6 Tell them they are going to listen to two children in the same situation. Play the tape.

7 Play the tape again and ask the children to repeat the dialogue.

8 In groups of three, using the tape dialogue as a model, the children have similar conversations substituting the relevant information taken from the map.

Tapescript
A I want to see stars and planets.
B Let's go to the Planetarium!
A Good idea! Excuse me, how do you get to the Planetarium?
C The Planetarium? Take the Underground to Baker Street. Outside the station turn right and go straight on, then turn right into Marylebone Road. The Planetarium is on the right next to Madame Tussaud's.

19 Write and describe.

Tell the children to imagine that they are writing to a penpal and giving him/her instructions on how to get to their house from the nearest station. If the children have problems remembering the street names, you could photocopy a town plan for them to use.

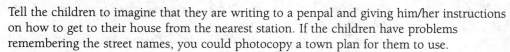

Drama time
2 New York (See page 10 of the Introduction for notes on *Drama time* for the story.)

TRAPPED IN SPACE!

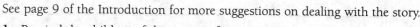

Story time

See page 9 of the Introduction for more suggestions on dealing with the story.

1 Remind the children of the story so far.

2 Focus attention on the title *Trapped in Space!*, and in L1 explain what this means. Ask the children what they think is taking place in this episode. Get them to look at the pictures and ask questions like *Where's Doctor Alpha?* Explain that Doctor Alpha is on the alien spaceship and Marla and Rui are explaining what has happened and that their computer is malfunctioning.

3 Focus attention on the computer screen and the words *SULPHUR, MERCURY, QUARTZ.* Ask if they know what these words mean and eventually explain them. Ask the children why they think the names of these materials appear on the computer screen. (These are the materials the aliens need to repair their spaceship.)

4 Point to the transmitter and remind the children that they have already seen this in the first episode, when Marla was helping Kanda into the capsule. Ask *What numbers are there on the transmitter?* (85, 37) *What letters are there on the transmitter?* (W, N) Ask *What do you think* (W, N) *are?* (West, North.) Ask them what they think the numbers indicate (*the location of the capsule*).

> **i** **LONGITUDE/LATITUDE: this might be a good moment to involve the children's knowledge of geography (if they have studied this particular aspect).**

5 Let the children study the rest of the pictures in Episode 3 for a while. Make sure that the children have understood that:

a Doctor Alpha has been transported up to the spaceship where Marla and Rui explain why they need his help.

b Marla, Rui and Doctor Alpha have located Kanda's capsule in the National Park in Kentucky, USA.

c the transmitter will enable them to locate Kanda's capsule.

d the materials have to be put in Kanda's capsule which, once reactivated, will return to the main spaceship.

e they haven't got enough energy to beam down both Doctor Alpha and the transmitter, so Doctor Alpha is left on the spaceship.

f Ben and his friends receive the transmitter and suddenly hear Doctor Alpha's voice.

g Doctor Alpha gives them instructions where to go but is cut off when he tries to tell them where to find the materials.

h the safety of Doctor Alpha, Kanda and the aliens now depends on Ben and his friends.

6 Tell the children that they are going to listen to the third episode of the story. Follow the *Story time* procedure on page 9 of the Introduction. Play the tape and ask the children to listen out for:

a the location of Kanda's capsule (*It's in the National Park in Kentucky*).

b the code Marla gives to Doctor Alpha to reactivate the capsule (*31.10*).

c the festival mentioned in the story (*Halloween*).

7 Ask the children to close their books and to decide whether the following statements are true or false. Play the tape once again.

1 Doctor Alpha says *Have you got a map of the Earth?* (T)

2 Ben says *I think it's a radio.* (T)

3 Ben says *We can hear you!* (F)

TRAPPED IN SPACE!

Lesson 1

OBJECTIVES:	to ask for and give opinions; to justify an opinion
TARGET LANGUAGE:	*What do you think it is/they are? / Why? I think it's a/ they're ... because ...*
RECYCLED LANGUAGE:	animals, simple descriptions, shapes, adjectives
PREVIEW:	*I don't know. You're a genius!*
MATERIALS:	cassette player, cassette 1, photocopies of resource page 132

Introduction

Remind your students of the moment in the story when the transmitter materialised in front of the children. Ask if Ben and his friends knew immediately that it was a transmitter. What did they think it was? (*a radio*)

1 Listen and repeat.

See page 13 of the Introduction for more information on the *Listen and repeat* activities.

1 Focus attention on the picture and the puzzled expressions on the children's faces. As Susan didn't know what the object was, she decided to ask Ben. Tell your students that they are going to learn how to ask for and give an opinion. Play the tape.

2 Mime and say *Repeat!* Play the tape again and get the children to repeat. Drill the sentences using choral and group drilling.

3 In pairs child A turns his/her back to child B who puts a familiar school or personal object in child A's hand and asks *What do you think it is?* Child A answers *I think it's a ... .*

4 When they have played this game, call out a child to the front of the class. Put two or three coloured pencils in his/her hand (behind his/her back) and ask the rest of the class if you can still ask the question *What do you think it is?* Elicit *What do you think they are?*

5 Let the children practise this form first and then get them to replay the game using both singular and plural objects.

2 Listen and point. Listen and draw.

1 Focus attention on the drawings and tell the children that they are going to play a similar game but this time using pictures instead of real objects.

2 Play the tape through once, then play A only. Ask the children to repeat the dialogue.

3 In pairs, the children use the model dialogue to ask about B. Play the tape for part B so that the children can check their answers and draw the object in the space provided.

4 Play part C, and the children use the model dialogue C to ask about the drawing in D. Play the tape for part D so that the children can check their answers and draw the objects in the space provided.

Tapescript

A

A Look at this! What do you think it is?
B Mmmm. I think it's a spaceship.
A No, it isn't. Wait ... now look!
B Ah. I think it's a dog.
A Yes, it is.

B

A Look at this! What do you think it is?
B Mmmm. I think it's a key.
A No, it isn't. Wait ... now look!
B Ah. I think it's a joystick.
A Yes, it is.

C

A Look! What do you think they are?
B I think they're houses.
A No, they aren't. Wait ... look now!
B Ah. I think they're pyramids!
A Yes, they are.

D

A Look! What do you think they are?
B I think they're apples.
A No, they aren't. Wait ... look now!
B Ah. I think they're oranges!
A Yes, they are.

5 Focus attention on the instructions under the drawings. Explain that they are going to play with their partner and draw their own outlines gradually adding details until their partner guesses.

3 Listen and point. Ask and answer.

This activity introduces the children to *why* and *because* in justifying their opinions. The solutions are provided on resource page 132.

1 Ask the children to look at the first picture. Play the tape and ask them to repeat the dialogue. Drill the sentences using choral and group drilling.

2 Ask the children if they agree: *Do you think it's a girl? Are you sure?* If you wish, you could show the children the solution for this particular picture so that they understand how the pictures may be misleading; this picture in fact shows a boy sitting on the sofa with his arm around his dog.

3 Continue with the other three prompts in the same way, and supply any vocabulary the children may need for their conclusions. Let the children do the activity in pairs and subsequently show them the cards from resource page 132 with the solutions.

Possible explanations

1 girl / long hair
2 hen / feathers
3 sun / round and yellow
4 polar bear / big / black nose / small eyes / etc.

Lesson 2

OBJECTIVES:	to ask about a scene and give a description (1)
TARGET LANGUAGE:	language of description
RECYCLED LANGUAGE:	*Who? / What? / Where? / When? / Why? Because ...* *on holiday, need*
MATERIALS:	cassette player, cassette 1

TRAPPED IN SPACE!

Introduction

The following activity consists of three parts. The objective is to help the children to move away from the single functional utterance towards a more sophisticated use of the language, i.e. description.

4 Look and read.

1 Ask the children what questions you ask when they look at a picture or sequence from the story. Elicit *Who's this? What is it? Where are they?* etc.

2 Focus attention on the question words and the associated drawings. Read out the question words one at a time getting the children to point to each one in turn.

> **WH- QUESTIONS: the use of *wh-* questions is frequent in L1 as a synthesis of information relating to an event or episode and to teach children how to build up a narrative. This activity could therefore strike a familiar chord with children who have followed this style of curriculum.**

4a Look at this picture and read.

1 This part presents a model of narrative passage based on a sequence of answers to *wh-* questions represented by the same symbols used in the previous activity. The children look at the drawing of Doctor Alpha and the children at the airport.

2 They then read all five pieces of information about the scene. Draw their attention to the fact that there is a symbol before each piece of information. Accept just the question words for the moment, e.g *Who? When?* etc.

4b Read and complete.

1 The children look at the second scene. Get them to identify the characters and where they are and what is happening.

2 The gapped passage this time contains questions and answers. Each gap is preceded by a small pictorial cue which will guide the children to produce either the question or the answer. Go through the activity orally with the class and then let the children complete the gaps.

Key

Who are they? They're *Marla* and *Rui*. *Where* are they? They're on a *spaceship* in the *solar-system*. *What* happens in the story? They send a *message* to Earth? *Why?* Because *they* need help.

Lesson 3

OBJECTIVES:	to ask about a scene and give a description (2)
TARGET LANGUAGE:	language of description
RECYCLED LANGUAGE:	*Who? / What? / Where? / When? / Why? Because ...*
MATERIALS:	cassette player, cassette 1

Introduction

Elicit the questions the children studied in the last lesson, e.g. *Who are they? Who's this? Where is it? Where are they?* etc.

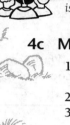

4c Match the answer with the right question.

1 Focus attention on the scene showing Doctor Alpha on the spaceship. The children read the questions and the answers as they appear on the page.
2 They then try to match the questions with the right answers. Check with the class.
3 As a final activity, using the questions to establish the order, the children read the answers and discover that they have a short story.

5 Work in pairs.

1 Focus the attention on the picture from the Student's Book that the two children in Activity 5 (page 28) are looking at.
2 On the left-hand side of the board write the question word in the order given, and then opposite each question write the following answer prompts, so the board looks like this:
When? (We don't know, so students can invent: *year 2238/morning/11 o'clock,* etc.)
Who?   Marla, Rui and Kanda
Where? spaceship/solar system/space/near Earth
What?   sending/helping/checking
Why?   Damek Za coming/wants to kill
3 Encourage the children to produce the complete questions and answers, e.g.
When is it?   *It's morning./It's eleven o'clock.*
Who are they?   *They're Marla, Rui and Kanda.*
Where are they?   *They're on a spaceship/in the solar system/in space/near Earth.*
What are they doing?   *They're sending Kanda to Earth/helping Kanda/checking the co-ordinates.*
Why?   *Because Damek Za is coming/wants to kill Kanda.*
4 The children now work in pairs asking and answering the questions.
5 Get the children to look at other scenes from the three episodes and talk about them in the same way. Explain that they need not ask all the questions, only those relevant to the scene they choose.

Extension: retelling old stories

It would be nice for the children to look again at the storyline pages in *Quest* 1 and *Quest* 2, to recall and to talk about various scenes. This could be done periodically as a relaxing activity which also provides the children with valuable recyling opportunities – it is also fun for them to remember Ben and Jasper's adventures!

TRAPPED IN SPACE!

Lesson 4

OBJECTIVES:	to ask about a scene and give a description (3); to build a narrative
TARGET LANGUAGE:	language of description and narratives
RECYCLED LANGUAGE:	*Who? / What? / Where? / When? / Why? Because ...*
MATERIALS:	cassette player, cassette 1, photocopies of resource page 133

6   GAME: The story wheel

See page 15 of the Introduction for more suggestions on dealing with games.

> **NARRATIVE BUILDING: this is a very useful cross-curricular activity in that it allows the children to depart from the single utterance phase in L2 and to approach a more mature way of expressing themselves. Moreover, the 5 Wh-questions system is normally used by other teachers in the team to teach how to build a text in their own language.**

1   Focus attention on the story wheel and give the children some time to study it. Explain that the storyline runs around the outside of the wheel and that the pictures/words on the inside are possible variations to a story.

2   Do a sample story with the class, eliciting suitable answers from the children. Say *Look! Daga is a (witch). She's very (ugly). She lives (in a dark forest). She (works a spell) every (day) because she wants to be a (mermaid).*

3   Focus attention on the *Whoosh!*, asking what has happened (*the wish has worked*). At this point suggest they continue using the same procedure thus creating a 'never-ending story' in which the end of one episode is the start of the next.

4   The children sit in groups of six. Each child chooses a part of the story (1, 2, 3, etc.). Child number 1 starts the story deciding how he/she wants to complete his/her sentence and so on until the story is finished.

5   They then draw in the bubble in the centre of the story wheel what the desired transformation would be (in this way the teacher can check comprehension).

6   Once they have experimented with the various storylines, focus attention on the question words below and ask them to find which sector of the story answers the questions.

Key

Who? (Daga is a ... ./She's very ... .)   Where? (She lives ... .)

What? (She kisses/speaks/works/plays ... .)   When? (Every ... .)

Why? (Because she wants to be a ... .)

Extension: story reconstruction from drawings

Form pairs of children by putting together children from different teams. Child A shows the other his/her drawing and Child B has to reconstruct the story from the drawing. The children write the story.

Extension: extend creativity in the storyline

To stimulate the use of imagination ask the children to expand some parts of the story giving prompts like:

Daga is a witch. What's the witch like? Is she tall/short/fat? Has she got white/black/green hair/eyes? Is she nice or nasty? Has she got a cat? What does she like? (bat's sweat/frog's blood ...) She lives in a castle. What's the castle like? Is it dark/big/small ... ? How many rooms are there? What's the witch's favourite room? Are there any animals in the castle? Who else lives in the castle? She plays a magic violin. What colour is it? Is it big/small? Where does she keep it? etc.

To do this activity the children can work in groups and produce a wall chart with illustrations and captions.

Extension: create new stories

To consolidate language further, working in groups the children produce drawings/words illustrating new characters and situations, e.g. *tiger/monster/elephant/little boy in a house/school/cave/on a hill/near a river/in a park*, etc.
Collect in the drawings from each group and put them on your desk face down in six piles. Following the usual order, call out a child (*Kim*) who chooses one card from the first pile (*monster*), holds it up and the class calls out, e.g. (*Kim*) *is a* (*monster*), and so on.

SONG: Luna

See page 9 of the Introduction for more information for dealing with songs and raps.

1 Hand out copies of resource page 133.
2 Ask the children to look at the drawings and identify them (they show a princess, a bird, a fairy, a queen, a dragon, a cat, a panther and a witch). Model and drill the new words.
3 Using the illustrations, explain that this song is about a magic mermaid called Luna. Luna feels restless beneath the sea and wants to use her magic powers to turn herself into someone (or something) else ... but what?
4 Using mime, explain that Luna has a magic spell which she sings every night as she plays her magic violin.
5 Tell the children they are going to listen to the song and they have to guess which characters Luna does NOT want to become (*a witch, a panther, a cat, a dragon*). Get the children to put up a hand and/or put a tick beside the relevant picture when they hear one of the characters mentioned (*princess, bird, queen, fairy*).

Extension: listen and fill the gaps

Once the children have grasped the idea of the song, you could put the words on the board gapping certain items that the children listen out for. e.g. *She wants to _____ near a lake. Every _____ she plays her violin*, etc. This will give them a simple task to do while they are learning the melody.

Drama time

3 Trapped in Space! (See page 10 of the Introduction for notes on *Drama time* for the story.)

REVISION

Lesson 1

OBJECTIVES:	to revise the language presented in Units 1–3
MATERIALS:	blank slips of paper

1 CROSSWORD: Read and complete.

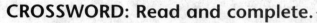

1 Ask the children what they can ask/say to you if they don't know a word in English or they have difficulty understanding or answering a question. Elicit *I don't know. I don't understand. What's this in (L1)? How do you say (money) in (L1)? How do you spell (money/it)?* etc.

2 Tell them that these are all sentences they can use if they find themselves in difficulties with the definitions, but that you want to see how far they can get without your help.

3 Focus attention on the small drawings surrounding the crossword and explain that these are also there to help them with the clues.

4 The children first do the crossword individually. Then ask them to check with their partners and discuss any discrepancies. During the checking phase they can ask their partners, e.g. *I don't understand number (3),* or *What's number (3)?* or *I don't know number (3).*

5 After they have checked together, check with the whole class.

Key

Across	Down
3 Saturn	1 hospital
5 system	2 bus
9 Rui	4 underground
10 camper	6 Mars
11 park	7 ship
14 bank	8 Jupiter
15 library	12 Mercury
16 museum	13 village

Extension: write your own crossword

In two teams or in small groups, using the clues as models, the children write their own variations of the clues provided, e.g. number 3 could be changed to *It's the planet with rings,* number 1 to *You go there when you are sick/ill,* etc. As some of the clues are not easily modified, each team or group should produce ten clues. When the clues are ready, the teams exchange their clues and try to answer. The first team to find all the correct solutions and write them on a sheet of paper will win.

STORING AND RE-USING QUIZ QUESTIONS: the slips of paper containing these quiz type questions can be stored in a large bottle/bowl/box and can be used for future treasure-hunt activities, warm-up activities or for establishing turns or lining-up, or can be given to children who are waiting for others to finish an activity.

Lesson 2

| OBJECTIVES: | to revise the language presented in Units 1–3 |
| MATERIALS: | cassette player, cassette 1, photocopies of resource pages 134–135, dice |

2 GAME: The golden planet

See page 15 of the Introduction for more suggestions on dealing with games.

1 Hand out copies of resource pages 134–135. The children colour and cut out the playing cards and while they are doing this they can familiarise themselves with the language content.

2 Explain that these cards are needed for a game and contain cues for producing language. Before cutting them out, go through the instructions on the cue cards with the children and check that they understand what is required. For the 'Compare' card, any suitable adjective is acceptable if used as a comparison.

3 Go through all the cards with the class and elicit all the possible answers for each card.

4 Let the children observe the board game in their books and explain the rules of the game:
  a the cards are shuffled and placed face down.
  b the player throws the dice. When he/she lands on a star or a planet, he/she takes a card and has to answer the question. When the player lands on an asteroid, he/she has to carry out the given instructions.
  c if the answer is correct the player may proceed to the next turn, if not, he/she must return to his/her previous position on the board.
  d when the cards are all used up, they are re-shuffled and re-used.
  e the winner is the first child to land on the golden planet.

Extension: new cards

The children can produce new cards for the game.

3 SONG: My home town

See page 15 of the Introduction for more information on dealing with songs and raps.

1 Hand out copies of resource page 136.

2 Give the children time to study the pictures. They will notice that there are three very similar towns showing various elements described in the song. Explain that only one illustration corresponds correctly to the song. The children have to listen and say which one it is.

Key

The correct illustration is the second one, which shows a house near a school, a swimming pool, a square, a bar, a church, a river, a park, some fields, the sun in the sky.

3 Once the children have done the task, teach them the song in the usual way.

REVISION

Storyboard

See page 11 of the Introduction for notes on the *Storyboard*.

This first session of *Storyboard* will create the first scenes of the wall frieze. Divide the children into small groups. Get each group to draw the main scenes from the first three episodes of the story. Each child in the group could concentrate on one scene. Before they start, check they have got the necessary material using classroom language to set up the activity. While the children are drawing, monitor the activity by saying *What's that? What are you doing? Who's this? Colour it carefully! That's nice/a bit small! Make it bigger/smaller!* etc. Once the children have drawn their scenes, they should draw speech bubbles that go with it. To consolidate the work they have done, encourage them to think of a simple descriptive sentence for each of their scenes, e.g. (for scenes from Unit 1):

Marla, Rui and Kanda are in their spaceship near planet Earth.
Damek Za attacks them.
Marla and Rui send Kanda to Earth.

If the children need any help with the speech bubbles, they can refer back to their books. You will need to help them with the descriptive sentences. A certain amount of interpretation should be allowed in their drawings to make the activity as creative as possible. The completed pictures, speech bubbles and descriptions are assembled together and stuck on the frieze.

SEARCH!

Story time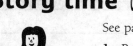

See page 9 of the Introduction for more suggestions on dealing with the story.

1 Remind the children of the story so far. Ask *Where's Doctor Alpha? (In the spaceship.) Where are Ben and his friends? (In America, in Otto's house.) What have they got? (A transmitter.) Why? (Because they want to find/Kanda/sulphur, mercury, quartz.)*

2 Focus attention on the title *Search!*, and in L1 explain what this means. Give them a few minutes to look at the pictures in the episode. Ask the children what they think is taking place.

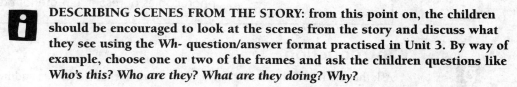

DESCRIBING SCENES FROM THE STORY: from this point on, the children should be encouraged to look at the scenes from the story and discuss what they see using the Wh- question/answer format practised in Unit 3. By way of example, choose one or two of the frames and ask the children questions like *Who's this? Who are they? What are they doing? Why?*

3 Focus attention on the first scene (5.1), and ask *What's Susan doing? (She's reading a book/an atlas.)* Ask *Why? (Because she wants to find the National Park.)* Ask them what they would take, to help them focus more closely on the rucksack.

4 Remind the class that Doctor Alpha told Ben and his friends to find three things in order to repair the spaceship (*sulphur, mercury and quartz*). Ask the children to look at the story and see if they think they have found any of these. Do not confirm or reject the suggestions for the moment.

5 Focus on scene 5.10 and ask why Susan is putting the thermometers in the rucksack. (*They contain mercury.*) In the following scene ask the children to identify the object in the shop window and then what the children are buying in the shop (*a chemistry set because it contains the materials they need*).

6 Let the children study the rest of the pictures in Episode 5 for a while. Make sure that the children have understood that:
   a Ben, Susan and Toby get ready to leave for the National Park.
   b they buy some thermometers because they contain mercury, and a chemistry set because it has got quartz and sulphur.
   c Ben buys the train ticket so that they can set off for Kentucky.

7 Follow the *Story time* procedure on page 9 of the Introduction. Play the tape and ask the children to follow the story in the book.

8 Play the tape again. This time they must listen out for:
   a the sort of shop they go in when Toby hurts his arm (*chemist's*).
   b the cost of the chemistry set (*$35*) and the cost of the tickets (*$300*).
   c what directions the policeman gives Susan to get to the station (*Go straight on, it's on your left*).

9 Ask the children to close their books and to decide whether the following statements are true or false. Play the tape once again.
   1 The co-ordinates are 85° North and 37° West. (F)
   2 Toby goes to the greengrocer's. (F)
   3 Susan says *Oh, Toby … there is a chemist's. Let's get some posters.* (F)
   4 Susan says *Excuse me, where's the station?* (T)

SEARCH!

Lesson 1

OBJECTIVES:	to discover new currencies; to handle prices, coins and banknotes
TARGET LANGUAGE:	English (and American) currency (*dollars, pounds, pence/p, coins, banknotes, money*)
RECYCLED LANGUAGE:	*How many ...?*, numbers
MATERIALS:	cassette player, cassette 1, blank slips of paper, photocopies of resource material page 137

Introduction

Ask the children if they know the names of any foreign currencies and in which countries they are used. Ask them if they know which currency is used in Britain and tell them that they are going to learn how to talk about British money.

1 Listen and point. Listen and repeat.

See page 13 of the Introduction for more information on the *Listen and repeat* activities.

1 Focus attention on the presentation flash. The children listen to the tape, point to the coins and banknotes. Explain that *p* is the abbreviation of *pence*.

Tapescript

A   Here's some American money. Here's some English money.
There are coins and banknotes. The first symbol means pounds. The second symbol means pence, but we say 'p'. There are one hundred pence in one pound.
B   Look at the coins. Listen and repeat.
A   One p ..., two p ... , five p ..., ten p ..., twenty p ..., fifty p ..., one pound ..., two pounds ...
B   Now look at the banknotes. Listen and repeat.
A   Five pounds ..., ten pounds ..., twenty pounds ..., fifty pounds

2 Play the tape again and ask the children to repeat.
3 Revise numbers by referring to the numbers on the tape and in the Student's Book.
4 Focus attention on the question *How many coins?* Tell the children they are going to listen to the prices shown. They listen and repeat.

Tapescript

Seventy-five p   twenty-five p   sixty-nine p   thirty-two p   forty-nine p   nine p

5 Now the children will have to decide which coins they need to make up these sums. The children have to write the minimum number of coins needed to make up the amount shown and say which coins they use. (Use the English money cut-outs from resource page 137 used in Activity 2 if you wish.)
6 For the second part, which includes both banknotes and coins, use the same procedure.

Tapescript

seven pounds forty-five p   sixteen pounds twenty-five p   two hundred and fifteen pounds, forty-six p   ninety-five p   six pounds thirty p   thirteen pounds.

52

2 PROJECT: Money

1 Hand out copies of resource page 137, and have the children cut out the coins and banknotes. The backs and fronts of the coins can be matched and stuck together.
2 Give the children instructions as to what colour the notes are, so that they can colour them in. Say *Look, this is five pounds. What colour is it? It's (light) blue. Colour it (light) blue!* The other notes are (approximately!) £10 orange/brown, £20 light violet, £50 red.

3 GAME: Bankrupt!

See page 15 of the Introduction for more suggestions on dealing with games. The aim of this game is to familiarise the children with the currency and to give them practice with numbers.

1 Put the children into small groups. Each child has two sets of coins/banknotes. The teacher has extra sets to change money if necessary.
2 Divide an A3 sheet of paper into twelve sectors. Write the value of each coin/banknote in the sectors.
3 Children throw a rubber, pencil sharpener, or something similar and small onto the sheet. Where it lands indicates the sum that must be paid to the player to the right. Model and drill the language the children can use during the game: *(10)p please! Here you are! Can you change ... ? I haven't got any change. Here's your change. Can I have (10)p, please?*
4 The game finishes when one of the children loses all his/her money!

Lesson 2

OBJECTIVES:	to ask about and give prices; to ask for something in a shop; to identify toys and games
TARGET LANGUAGE:	*Can I help you? I'd like a/some ..., please. Here you are. How much is it?* toys (*electronic pen, paints, make-up set, magic diary, batteries, water bombs, solar system mobile*), *a/an, some*
RECYCLED LANGUAGE:	money
MATERIALS:	cassette player, cassette 1

Introduction

In L1 elicit the language used in shops between shopkeepers and customers, and then remind the children of the story when Ben and his friends bought the chemistry set.

4 Listen and repeat.

See page 13 of the Introduction for more information on the *Listen and repeat* activities.

1 Ask the children to look at the presentation flash. Play the tape and tell them to listen and say if Ben is in England or America and how they found the answer. (*Ben is in a toy shop in England. He pays in pounds.*)
2 The class is divided into two teams. One team plays Ben and the other the shopkeeper. Then they swap over.
3 Play the tape again and ask the children to repeat one scene at a time, so that they can practise each model sentence.

SEARCH!

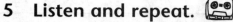

5 Listen and repeat.

See page 13 of the Introduction for more information on the *Listen and repeat* activities.

1 Focus attention on the catalogue. Ask the children if they recognise these toys. Tell them they're going to learn their names. Play the tape and ask the children to listen and repeat.

Tapescript

Here are some other toys. Listen and repeat.

an electronic pen	some paints	a make-up set
a magic diary	some batteries	some water bombs
some tennis balls	a solar system mobile	a tennis racket

2 As these names will be needed for the next activity, the children will have to be confident in using them. So consolidate with choral drilling and look-and-point practice.

3 Point out a toy in the catalogue. The children name it. After one or two examples choose a plural form. Underline the plural aspect and elicit from the children the reason why there is the word *some* instead of *a*.

4 The children close their books and, in pairs, they try to remember the toys in the catalogue.

Extension: in a toy shop

Tell the children that they are now going to ask for these items in the toy shop. The children practise the first exchange of the dialogue in pairs using the toys as prompts, e.g.

A *Can I help you?* **B** *I'd like a (solar system mobile) please.*
A *Here you are.* **B** *Thank you.*

6 Listen and write the prices.

Focus attention on the small price tags on the catalogue and explain to the children that they must listen to the prices and write them next to the appropriate tags.

Tapescript

an electronic pen   five pounds
some paints   eight pounds, forty p
a make-up set   six pounds fifty-five p
a magic diary   fifteen pounds
some batteries   one pound, twenty-five p
some water bombs   three pounds, ten p
some tennis balls   five pounds ninety-nine p
a solar system mobile   seven pounds eighty-five p
a tennis racket   seventy pounds

Lesson 3

OBJECTIVES:	to talk about shops and items sold; to distinguish between countable and uncountable nouns
TARGET LANGUAGE:	Shops (*greengrocer's, baker's, butcher's, newsagent's chemist's, toy shop, grocer's, sports shop, optician's, clothes shop*), food (*lemonade, ham, cherries, bread, strawberries, crisps*), holidays (*tent, suncream, camera, swimming costume, rucksack, video camera*), *some/any, need*
RECYCLED LANGUAGE:	*have got, eggs, ice cream, apples, fish, potatoes, I'd like …, please. / How much …?, money*
PREVIEW:	first conditional (*If it's raining, I'll read my book.*), present continuous to express future, *I like + -ing*
MATERIALS:	cassette player, cassette 1, photocopies of resource page 138, old magazines

Introduction

Talk about the last weekend/recent school holiday(s), and ask the children if any of them went anywhere special. Encourage them to tell you what they took with them, and where they would like to go if they could go on a weekend trip somewhere or if they had a day off school. Suggest, model and drill *the seaside, a picnic/camping trip, into the mountains/hills, have a party*, etc.

7 Listen and write the names.

1 Tell the children to open their books at page 38. Focus attention on the three children and explain that two of them are preparing their bags before going on holiday.

2 Introduce the three children, Becky, Tim and Paula. Model and drill the names so that the children will recognise them when they hear the tape. Write their names on the board.

3 Write *going to the seaside, camping in the mountains* and *having a party* on the board and tell the children that B, P and T are each involved in one of the three activities. They have to guess which one.

4 Play the tape and ask the children to listen and write the names of the three children in the spaces provided.

Tapescript

One

Becky   Hello. My name's Becky. I'm going on holiday. Look at my bed! I've got a lot of things ready. I've got some shorts and some T-shirts. I've got a hat and my sunglasses because it's very hot and sunny there; but if it's raining I'll read my book in the hotel. I've got my video-camera and … oh yes!! I've got some water bombs … for my brother!

Two

Tim   Hello! My name's Tim. It's my birthday tomorrow and my friends are coming to my house. I've got a lot of things ready. I've got a big cake, some ice cream, some bananas and strawberries. I've got some biscuits and some crisps … oh, and I've got a stereo – we can listen to music and dance!

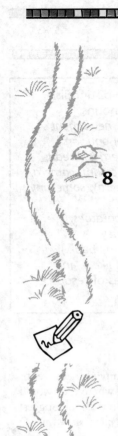

Three

Paula Hello, I'm Paula! I'm going on holiday. I love the mountains! Look on my bed! There are some pullovers and jeans; I've got an anorak and a cap and my sunglasses. I like walking so I've got my boots, a map and my 'walkman' because I like listening to music when I'm walking.

5 Play the tape again and ask them to listen and then say where the children are going.
6 Play the tape again and ask them to listen and identify the objects belonging to each child.

8 Listen and repeat. Write B, P or T.

See page 13 of the Introduction for more information on the *Listen and repeat* activities.

1 Tell the children they are going to learn the names of other things that Becky, Tim and Paula have to buy. Play the tape.

Tapescript

some lemonade a tent some ham some bread a comic some suncream a swimming costume some plasters some cherries a camera

2 Play the tape again and ask the children to repeat.
3 Now they have to decide who needs which object and write his/her initial in the box next to each word.
4 Play the tape once again to let the children check their answers.

Tapescript

Listen and check. Becky's going to the shops, because she needs a swimming costume and some suncream.

Tim is going to the shops, because, for the party, he needs some lemonade, some ham and some bread for the sandwiches, and some cherries ... because he likes them!

Paula is going to the shops because she wants to buy a tent for her mountain camping holiday. She hasn't got a camera, and she also needs some plasters and a comic ... she can read it if the weather is bad!

GAME: Memory test

Ask the children to close the book and to remember any of the objects. Now the children try and remember specific objects, e.g. *What's the first/last object? What are the red object(s)? What's the second object? What's the biggest object?* etc.

9 Listen and repeat. Listen and answer.

See page 13 of the Introduction for more information on the *Listen and repeat* activities.

1 Tell the children that these are the shops where Becky, Paula and Tim are going to get the things they need. Check that they recognise all of them in L1, and using ordinals ask them what the first/second, etc. shop sells. They should recognise the items displayed in the shop windows.
2 They then listen to the tape and repeat the names of the shops.

Tapescript

greengrocer's baker's butcher's newsagent's chemist's clothes shop optician's sports shop grocer's toy shop

3 Tell the children they are going to listen to someone asking where the children can buy their articles for their holidays. Warn them that they might be surprised to learn where certain things are sold! (This theme will be developed in the following **Escape Door** section, so discussion may be postponed.) They should answer when they hear *At the ...* which is their cue to call out the name of the shop or shops. Some have more than one correct answer.

Tapescript

A Where can Paula buy some plasters?
B At the ... At the chemist's.
A Where can Paula buy a tent?
B At the ... At the sports shop.
A Where can Paula buy a camera?
B At the ... At the chemist's.
A Where can Paula buy a comic?
B At the ... At the newsagent's.
A Where can Tim buy some lemonade?
B At the ... At the grocer's. or At the newsagent's.
A Where can Tim buy some ham?
B At the ... At the butcher's. or At the grocer's.
A Where can Tim buy some bread?
B At the ... At the baker's. or At the grocer's.
A Where can Tim buy some cherries?
B At the ... At the greengrocer's.
A Where can Becky buy a swimming costume?
B At the ... At the clothes shop. or At the sports shop.
A Where can Becky buy some suncream?
B At the ... At the chemist's.

4 Ask the children other questions using the items on the page, e.g. *Where can you buy an anorak?*

Escape door: shopping in Britain

Ask the children to compare these shops with the shops in their own country. *Do they sell the same things?* Elicit goods and different shops and if appropriate present these new names of shops. *Can you buy the same things in the same shops?* E.g. in some countries you can buy a camera/video camera/binoculars at the optician's, but in the UK this is not the case; you buy a camera at the chemist's or at the photographer's, or electrical goods shop.

10 SONG: Where's Mum?

See page 15 of the Introduction for more suggestions on dealing with songs and raps.

1 Hand out copies of resource page 138 and focus attention on the drawings and the items on the shopping list. Explain that the child in the song is looking for someone: *Who is it?* (Mum).
2 Tell the children they are going to listen to a song about shopping. Play the tape and let them listen to the words of the chorus, so that they get familiar with this section before progressing to the verses.
3 Play the tape again and ask them to listen and identify the shops mentioned and the articles purchased and not purchased.

SEARCH!

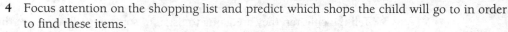

4 Focus attention on the shopping list and predict which shops the child will go to in order to find these items.

5 Ask the children to substitute the shop/shopkeeper and sing their 'own' verses.

11 Listen and repeat. Guess the shop.

See page 13 of the Introduction for more information on dealing with the *Listen and repeat* activities.

This activity is like a guessing game played in groups. One child in the group chooses a shop but doesn't tell the other children in the group which it is. This child is the shopkeeper. The others have to guess which shop it is by asking the shopkeeper for various items and by process of elimination they can guess which shop it is.

1 Focus attention on the dialogue in the book so that the children understand how the activity works. Tell the children they are going to listen to the model dialogue.

2 Play the tape once, the children then listen and repeat.

3 Model and drill *Sorry! I haven't got any.*

12 PROJECT: Make a shop.

1 In groups the children reproduce the shop window and sign of one of the following shops: *greengrocer's, grocer's* or *newsagent's.*

2 Then get them to cut out relevant items for their shop from magazines and 'put' them in the shop window together with a name/price tag, e.g. *potatoes: £2 a bag,* etc.

3 When the posters are ready the children 'play shop' by putting a desk in front of the poster and using the English money they cut out in Unit 5 Lesson 1.

> **ℹ** **ITEMS SOLD IN THE SHOPS: newsagent's: newspapers, magazines, comics, postcards, stamps, pens, pencils, rubbers, exercise books, writing paper, notebooks, chocolate bars and sweets, soft drinks, crisps, cheap toys, batteries, films, maps; (cigarettes, tobacco, matches, cigars, fireworks are also sold, but not to children under sixteen years of age).**
> **greengrocer's: fresh fruit and vegetables, packets of dried fruits and vegetables (not tinned usually), flowers.**
> **grocer's: tinned food, bread, packets of cakes, biscuits, tea, coffee, sugar, salt, frozen food, sweets and soft drinks, bacon, ham, cheese, milk, pasta, rice, etc.**

13 Listen and choose.

1 There are three shopping lists. The children listen to the tape and number them according to the order they hear them. They then match the list to the total shown on the bill extract.

Tapescript

One

Ben	Hello, Susan. I'm just going to the supermarket.
Susan	Can I come with you? I need some things ...
Ben	OK. ... Right. Where's my shopping list? Here it is ... I need some apples ... mmm ... these are nice. Dad likes red apples, but I like green! And potatoes ... Wow! This bag of potatoes is very heavy! That's all here ... Now, I want some fish.
Susan	It's over there, near the bread ...
Ben	Good, I need some bread, too ... I like brown bread ...

Susan	Yuk! I don't! What's next on your list?
Ben	Oh, good. Toffees! Me and Dad eat a lot when we watch TV! Mmm. These are my favourite … . OK. That's all the food finished. Now … I need some things for school.
Susan	What do you need?
Ben	Let's see … . A red pen, a blue pen and an exercise book.
Susan	Look. They're over there, near the toys. Let's go and get them.
Ben	How much is it, please?
Cashier	That's twenty-one pounds, fifty-five, please.
Ben	… Twenty, twenty-one, and here's fifty-five pence.
Cashier	Thanks. … 'Bye.

Two

Grocer	Good morning, Toby!
Toby	Good morning, Mr. Hogg. I'd like some things for my mum, please.
Grocer	OK. Have you got a list?
Toby	Yes … somewhere … right … I'd like a packet of ham, please.
Grocer	Ham … here you are. Anything else?
Toby	Can I have some bread … some eggs … and some ice cream.
Grocer	Chocolate, strawberry or vanilla ice cream, Toby?
Toby	Mmm, … I like strawberry … oh, strawberry ice cream, please.
Grocer	Anything else?
Toby	Yes … have you got any pens and exercise books?
Grocer	Yes, look, they're over there on the left …
Toby	OK. Two pens and an exercise book … that's all, I think. No, wait! Very important … I'd like some toffees, please!
Grocer	Of course! Right … bread, eggs, ham, toffees, ice cream, two pens and an exercise book … that's twenty-five pounds, fifty-five pence, please, Toby.
Toby	Here you are.
Grocer	Here's your change … . Thank you. 'Bye, Toby.
Toby	'Bye, Mr. Hogg.

Three

Mum	Susan! Can you help me with the shopping?
Susan	Oh, no! Right, Mum. I'm coming.
Mum	This new supermarket is so big!
Susan	Have you got your list, Mum?
Mum	Yes, … here it is … right, Susan, bread, fish, potatoes, ham, and … mmm … these must be for you, I think, an electronic pen, some batteries and some toffees … OK. Susan, can you get your things and some bread, please. It's over there next to the toys.
Susan	White bread?
Mum	No, get some brown.
Susan	Why?
Mum	Because Dad doesn't like white bread.
Susan	OK.
Mum	I'll get some fish, potatoes and ham … let's meet at the checkout …
Cashier:	That's thirty-five pounds, twenty-five pence, please.
Mum	Here you are … thank you.
Cashier	Bye.

2 Ask the children to work out the following sums: if the people all pay with a £50 note, how much change will each get?

SEARCH!

Lesson 4

OBJECTIVES:	to describe how to get to places; to describe and talk about shopping facilities; to find out about famous British shops
TARGET LANGUAGE:	shops (*computer shop, pet shop, department store*), *go past/along*
RECYCLED LANGUAGE:	shops, facilities, directions, products, locations, superlatives, prepositions of place
PREVIEW:	*There's one ..., anything, another*
MATERIALS:	cassette player, cassette 1

Introduction

Ask the children about the facilities in their town. Ask them what shops there are near the school and elicit *It's near/opposite/next to the bank/police station*, etc.

14 Listen and match. Find the shops.

1   Focus attention on the shop signs and identify them with the class. Tell them that these shops are to be found in the town centre shown on the map.
2   Focus attention on the street map. Familiarise the children with the map by asking some questions, e.g. *Where's the library?* Encourage the children to answer using the names of the streets, and where appropriate with the position, e.g. *It's in Parker Lane./It's opposite the supermarket.*
3   Tell the children they are going to listen to the tape and, starting from the station, follow the instructions and discover where the shops are, writing the corresponding number on the map. Tell the children to do this in pencil as the map will be used again later.

Tapescript

One
Man	Excuse me! How do you get to *Point and Click*?
Woman	*Point and Click*? What's that?
Man	It's a large computer shop.
Woman	Oh yes! I know. Go straight on, turn right into Bridge Lane, go past the Post Office, and the computer shop is there ... between the Post Office and the bank.
Man	Thank you very much. Bye.

Two
Girl	Excuse me. Where can I get some dog food?
Boy	There's a pet shop in Burnley Road ...
Girl	Where is it, please?
Boy	Well, go straight on, go past the police station ... turn right ... that's Burnley Road ... the pet shop is on your left, opposite the police station.
Girl	Thank you.
Boy	That's OK.

Three
Boy	Excuse me. Is there a baker's near here?
Woman	A baker's ... yes, there's one in Parker Lane.

Boy	Is it far?
Woman	No ... turn left here, then turn right into Queen's Park Road ... .
Boy	Queen's Park Road ... yes, ... then?
Woman	Turn right again. That's Parker Lane. The baker's is next to the supermarket ...
Boy	Thank you. Bye.

Four

Boy	Can you see the toy shop?
Girl	No, I can't. Let's ask this lady ... . Excuse me!
Woman	Yes. What's the matter?
Girl	Well, there's a toy shop near here but I don't know where it is!
Woman	Oh, yes. *Kids World* ... I know it. It's not far from here. ... Turn right here and then turn left into Harold Street. Turn left into Bridge Lane and the toy shop is there, opposite the bank.
Girl	Opposite the bank? Thank you.
Woman	That's all right. Goodbye.

Five

Man	Excuse me. Is there a newsagent's near here?
Boy	The nearest one is in Parker Lane ... go straight on and turn left. The newsagent's is on the corner opposite the supermarket.
Man	Opposite the supermarket ... thanks. Bye.
Boy	Bye.

Six

Woman	Excuse me. I need a chemist's ...
Man	Yes ... there's a new chemist's shop now.
Woman	How do I get there please?
Man	Go straight on along North Street ... past the swimming pool and the police station ... turn right into Burnley Road.
Woman	Burnley Road?
Man	Yes ... there's a pet shop ... go past the school, and the chemist's is on your left, next to the school.
Woman	Thank you very much.
Man	That's all right. Bye.

4 Ask the children to rub out the pencilled numbers from the previous activity and write new numbers on each in order to reposition the shops where they like.

5 The children work in pairs. Give each child a shopping list which includes two or three articles from the various shops. Their task is to buy the items, and to do this they have to find out where the shops are, by asking their partners.

6 Model the activity with the class, and as you elicit the dialogue write it on the board so that the children will have a model dialogue to refer to during the substitution activity.

15 Describe the shops near your house.

1 Tell the children they are going to describe some of the shops near their homes.

2 Read the questions in the book with the class and by eliciting the information, build up the text on the board by answering the questions, e.g. *I live in* (name of road). *The nearest shop is a* (name of shop) *called* (trade name). *To get there, you* (directions and location). *Near my house there is also a* baker's/chemist's/grocer's. *I can buy* (names of items) *at the* (name of shop). *The* (name of shop) *is opposite/near* (name of a well known place).

3 The children write the description and, if you wish, they could also draw a small map to illustrate the description.

SEARCH!

16 Let's go shopping!

1 Ask the children if they remember the biggest shop they have ever been in. Ask them what was on sale and how many floors it had. Tell them that in many places, as well as the usual shops (elicit the names), there are also very large shops called stores or department stores. Some of these are famous all over the world for different reasons.

2 Focus attention on the *Culture Vulture* page. There are three photos of famous shops in London: Harrods, Hamley's and the Disney Store. Next to each photo there is a description which explains what kind of shop it is, what you can buy there, and where it is.

3 Tell the children they are going to listen to these descriptions. They listen and follow in their books.

Tapescript

Harrods is the biggest shop in Britain. It's a department store. You can buy anything there, from a pen to an elephant. It's in Brompton Road.

Hamley's is a very famous toy shop. It's the biggest toy shop in Europe. There are six floors with hundreds and hundreds of toys. It's in Regent Street.

Let's go out of Hamley's, turn left, go straight on. On the left there's another famous shop, the Disney Store. There are T-shirts, costumes, videos, toys and computer games – all with your favourite Disney characters.

4 Write the following statements on the board and ask the children whether they are true or false.
1 Harrods is a small shop. (F)
2 Harrods is the biggest toy shop in Europe. (F)
3 You can buy a teddy bear at Hamley's. (T)
4 There are hundreds and hundreds of floors at Hamley's. (F)
5 Hamley's is in Regent Street. (T)
6 The Disney Store is opposite Hamley's. (F)
7 You can buy a Hercules costume at The Disney Store. (T)

Drama time

5 Search! (See page 10 of the Introduction for notes on *Drama time* for the story.)

THE LOST RUCKSACK

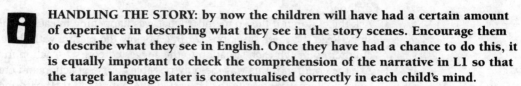

Story time

See page 9 of the Introduction for more suggestions on dealing with the story.

1 Remind the children of the story so far. Focus attention on the title *The Lost Rucksack*, and in L1 explain what this means. Ask the children what they think is going to take place in this episode.

2 Get them to look at the pictures in this episode. Ask the children what they think is taking place.

> **HANDLING THE STORY:** by now the children will have had a certain amount of experience in describing what they see in the story scenes. Encourage them to describe what they see in English. Once they have had a chance to do this, it is equally important to check the comprehension of the narrative in L1 so that the target language later is contextualised correctly in each child's mind.

3 Let the children study the rest of the pictures for a while. Make sure they have understood that:
   a the children have arrived at the National Park.
   b they use the transmitter to find out which direction to go.
   c the children follow Jasper believing that he has found the way to the capsule.
   d Jasper has, in fact, led the children to a scout/guide camp.
   e Ben and his friends have lunch with the scouts before setting off to find the capsule.
   f when they are near a large cave, the signal from the transmitter becomes stronger.
   g because of the darkness, they need a torch and so Toby goes to get it from Ben's rucksack.
   h the children realise that, on leaving the camp, Ben picked up the wrong rucksack.
   i the mercury is in Ben's rucksack back at the camp.
   j they decide to go back but suddenly a bear appears blocking their exit.

4 Follow the *Story time* procedure on page 9 of the Introduction. Play the tape and ask the children to follow the story on the book.

5 Play the tape again. This time they must listen out for:
   a information about Mammoth Cave (*It's the biggest cave in America*).
   b what Toby says when he realises that the rucksack is not Ben's (*This isn't your rucksack!*).
   c which of the three minerals is in Ben's rucksack (*mercury*).
   d what Ben says when he decides to return to the campsite (*Let's go back!*).

Lesson 1

OBJECTIVES:	to make suggestions with *Let's ...* and *Shall ...* and accept/refuse them
TARGET LANGUAGE:	*What shall we do? Let's ..., Me too.*
RECYCLED LANGUAGE:	verbs of action
MATERIALS:	cassette player, cassette 1

Introduction

Remind the children that Ben, Susan and Toby often found themselves in difficulty and were

THE LOST RUCKSACK

unsure about what to do. Explain that in the last episode this happened three times, and each time one of them suggested a possible course of action.

1 Listen and repeat. Read and match.

See page 13 of the Introduction for more information on the *Listen and repeat* activities.

1 Focus the attention on the pictures and tell the children they are going to listen to the tape twice. The first time, accompany the text and explain the meaning through mime.
2 The second time get the children to repeat. Drill the sentences using choral and group drilling.
3 Ask the children if they remember what was happening in each of these excerpts from the story. Read the three situations (A, B, C) below the picture with the class and then ask the children to match each situation to the suggested course of action in the storyline.
4 Ask the children if this was the only possible course of action and encourage them to suggest alternatives. Write the suggested alternatives on the board, helping with any lexis. (e.g. *Let's go in, Let's ask the Park Ranger, Let's ask for information, Let's look at the park shop, Let's send Jasper in first, Let's look in the rucksack,* etc.) This activity, as well as encouraging the children to find different solutions to a problem, will prepare the ground for the next activity.

2 Listen and repeat. Listen and number.

See page 13 of the Introduction for more information on the *Listen and repeat* activities.

1 Focus attention on the drawings. Explain that they all illustrate different suggestions in each situation. Go through the scenes with the children clarifying where necessary what is happening and what the suggestion is.
2 Play the tape and ask the children to listen and repeat the dialogues.

Tapescript

A	What shall we do?	B	Let's watch TV.
A	What shall we do?	B	Let's play Monopoly.
A	What shall we do?	B	Let's go to the cinema.
A	What shall we do?	B	Let's go out.
A	What shall we do?	B	Let's have a Coke.
A	What shall we do?	B	Let's have an ice cream.
A	What shall we do?	B	Let's watch a video.
A	What shall we do?	B	Let's telephone Dad.
A	What shall we do?	B	Let's play volleyball.
A	What shall we do?	B	Let's use the computer.

3 Explain that they are going to listen to five short dialogues in which children are making suggestions. They have to listen for and number the situation that corresponds to the children's final decision.

Tapescript

One
A It's a lovely day. It's nice and sunny. What shall we do?
B Let's go out!
A Good idea!

Two
A Ufff! I'm bored. What shall we do?

B Let's watch TV.
A Oh no! ... It's 8 o'clock, there's the News. I don't like the News!
B Let's watch a video, then!
A Good idea!

Three

A What's the matter?
B Look! My bicycle is broken! I can't go home!
A What shall we do?
B Let's telephone Dad!

Four

A What's the matter?
B I've got a lot of history homework.
A Can I help you?
B Yes. Thanks. I can't find any information about Egypt.
A Let's use the computer!
B Good idea!

Five

A Great goal! Well done!
B Thanks! Whew! I'm hot! ... and thirsty!
A Me too.
B Let's have a Coke!
A Yes!

3 Ask and answer.

1 Set a scene, e.g. *Oh dear ... it's raining today! What shall we do?* and invite suggestions from the children using appropriate alternatives, such as *Let's watch TV!/Let's use the computer!*
2 Write on the board different scene settings, e.g.

1 *It's raining.*	2 *It's sunny.*
3 *You're thirsty.*	4 *You're hungry.*
5 *You're bored.*	6 *You're out and your bicycle breaks.*
7 *Your cousin arrives.*	8 *You're on the beach.*

3 In pairs, the children look at the board and one of them chooses a number which sets the scene and asks *What shall we do?* The other child offers an appropriate suggestion.

Extension: making a second suggestion

At a further level you could extend the dialogue and get the children to refuse the first suggestion so that the first child has to offer a second alternative, e.g.

A *What shall we do?*
B *Let's have a coke!*
A *No, I don't like coke!*
B *OK. Let's have a (Sprite)!*
A *OK.*

THE LOST RUCKSACK

Lesson 2

OBJECTIVES:	to talk about camping
TARGET LANGUAGE:	camping vocabulary (*sleeping bag, blanket, cup, plate, fork, knife, spoon, pan, towel, soap, toilet paper*)
RECYCLED LANGUAGE:	*have got, some, tent*
PREVIEW:	*everything*
MATERIALS:	cassette player and cassette 1, photocopies of resource pages 139–141

Introduction

1 Remind the children of the scouts that Ben and his friends met in the National Park. Ask the children if any of them have ever been camping. *Where? Do you like camping? What's exciting/boring about camping? Are you frightened at night? What do you eat? Do you help cook? Where do you sleep?*

2 Tell the children to imagine they are preparing for a camping holiday. Ask what they would take with them. Accept all offers for the moment. Tell the children that they are going to learn the names of some of these things in English.

4 Listen and repeat.

See page 13 of the Introduction for more information on the *Listen and repeat* activities.

1 Focus attention on the picture and tell the children that the child is going to a summer camp. Explain that the child's father reads the item he will need for the camp, and the child looks for it. Play the tape and ask the children to point to the numbered objects.

Tapescript

Dad	OK. Let's see if you've got everything.
Child	OK, Dad. Go on ... .
Dad	One. A tent.
Child	A tent. OK.
Dad	Two. A sleeping bag.
Child	A sleeping bag. OK.
Dad	Three. A blanket.
Child	A blanket. OK.
Dad	Four. A cup.
Child	A cup. OK.
Dad	Five. A plate.
Child	A plate. OK.
Dad	Six. A fork.
Child	A fork. OK.
Dad	Seven. A knife.
Child	A knife. OK.
Dad	Eight. A spoon.
Child	A spoon. OK.
Dad	Nine. A pan.

Child A pan. OK.
Dad   Ten. A towel.
Child A towel. OK.
Dad   Eleven. Some soap.
Child Some soap. OK.
Dad   Twelve. Some toilet paper.
Child Some toilet paper. OK.
Dad   That's it! You've got everything!

2 Mime and say *Repeat!* Play the tape and ask the children to repeat. As there are several items, it is advisable to deal with them three or four at a time.

> **COUNTABLE/UNCOUNTABLE NOUNS: as *soap* and *toilet paper* are uncountable nouns in English, *some* is needed in place of the article. If you prefer to limit your practice to only countable nouns during this phase, *a bar of soap* and *a roll of toilet paper* can be taught instead.**

5 Test your memory.

1 In pairs the children look at the scene for two minutes then they close their books and try to remember as many objects as possible, scoring one point for each one correctly remembered.
2 Check comprehension and pronunciation asking *What's this? What's number (two)? What colour's the (soap)? Where's the (knife)? (Between the fork and the spoon.) What's next to the (cup)?*
3 Encourage the children to ask and answer similar questions about the camping items. In pairs, child A, with the book open, can ask questions about the objects. Child B tries to answer and then asks A a question.

6 Read and match.

The children read the items on the summer camp list and write the corresponding number referring back to the drawing in Activity 4.

7 GAME: Let's go camping!

See page 15 of the Introduction for more suggestions on dealing with games.

1 Hand out copies of resource pages 139–140. Explain to the children that they are going to play a game in which they have to match a drawing with the appropriate word card.
2 For this game you need only 24 cards. You don't need to cut out the last five cards, since these will be used in Activity 13. Each card represents either one of the numbered items in Activity 4 or the name of an object. Of the 24 cards needed for this game, 12 are pictures and 12 are matching word cards. The aim of the game is to make pairs.
3 Read through the words on the cards with the class before starting the game and ask the children to colour in the objects and back them (so they are not identifiable against the light and also so that they can be re-used).
4 Divide the class in groups of four. Each group has a complete set of 24 cards. Explain the rules of the game:
   a each group has to shuffle the cards and deal them out, six per child.
   b the first player chooses one of the other three players and asks him/her *Have you got a/some ...?*
   c if the child asked has either the drawing of this object or the word card he/she must hand it to the player who asked for it, saying *Yes, I have. Here you are.*

d if he/she has neither he/she answers *No, I haven't.*

e the child with the most pairs wins.

5 Remind the children of the classroom language associated with games, like *It's my turn, Don't cheat! You can't do that! It's not fair,* etc.

8 SONG: Camping

See page 15 of the Introduction for more information on dealing with songs and raps.

1 Hand out copies of resource page 141 and tell the children that this is the text of the song they are going to listen to.
2 Play the tape and ask the children to identify the names of the characters.
3 Play the tape again and let the children listen and repeat the refrain.
4 Play the tape once again and teach one verse at a time, then gradually build up the whole song by going back over the previous verse.

9 Play with the words.

These are simple word games to focus the attention on the written form.

GAME: Hangman

1 In this game you think of a word that the children have to guess, e.g. *tent.* Draw a dash for each letter on the board.
2 The children take turns in calling out a letter of the alphabet and, if correct, the letter is written in place of the appropriate dash. If it isn't, draw one piece of gallows on the board. At each successive incorrect guess, another piece is added to the gallows until the drawing is complete. At this stage you have won!
3 Once one or two letters have been guessed correctly, the children can try and call out what they think the right word is. If they guess it before the drawing is completed, they win.

GAME: Anagram bubbles

Choose one of the words from the cards used in Activity 7, and write each letter of that word in a circle, in random order. If you want to make it a little more challenging, write the letters of two of the words in each bubble!

GAME: Mystery letters

Write on the board the following letters: *k t p s e* and tell the children to write as many words as they can that contain any of these letters (not an anagram!)

GAME: Read and mime

The children pick one of the word cards from Activity 7 and mime an action that involves the use of the object shown. (If you prefer, you might like to remove the *toilet paper* card!)

Lesson 3

<table>
<tr><td>OBJECTIVES:</td><td>to talk about camping activities; to describe what is happening/what people are doing</td></tr>
<tr><td>TARGET LANGUAGE:</td><td>camping vocabulary (putting up a tent, washing up, cooking, going for a walk, having a shower, making something, collecting litter, climbing a rope, riding), Take your litter home!</td></tr>
<tr><td>RECYCLED LANGUAGE:</td><td>present continuous (she's swimming)</td></tr>
<tr><td>PREVIEW:</td><td>must</td></tr>
<tr><td>MATERIALS:</td><td>cassette player and cassette 1, photocopies of resource pages 139–140</td></tr>
</table>

Introduction

Reintroduce the theme of camping and revise the items the children learnt in the previous lesson. Introduce *litter*.

10 Listen and name.

1 Focus attention on the picture on page 48. Point out and help the children to identify the two people talking in the background of the picture (*the Park Ranger and the Camp Leader*).

2 Give the children some time to look at the various scenes and familiarise themselves with what's happening. Ask what the children are wearing (*shorts, shirts, shoes, socks, T-shirts, jackets*, etc.) in order to revise articles of clothing ready for the first activity.

3 Tell the children they are going to hear some information about what each child is wearing and what equipment is being used, and then they have to write the children's names in the boxes next to each child.

4 Write the names of the children camping on the board: *Tony, Anna, Ralph, Paula, Marco, Sandy, Eric, Tammy, Kathy, Ted, Conny*

Tapescript

Leader Oh, hello, Ranger.
Ranger Hello, Linda. You've got a lot of children here this time!
Leader Yes. They're very good!
Ranger What are their names?
Leader Well … can you see the two children over there? They're wearing orange T-shirts. They're collecting litter with that big bag. They're Tony and Anna.
Ranger Oh yes! They're doing a very good job!
Leader Yes. They're taking the bag to Ralph. He's wearing a red T-shirt, and he's making something from an old plastic bottle. He's got some glue and scissors.
Ranger Mmm! Very clever! Who's that?
Leader You mean Paula?
Ranger She's wearing green shorts. She's putting up a tent.
Leader Oh, yes, that's Paula. Now, the kitchen area is over there.
Ranger What a lot of dirty plates, cups, knives and forks!
Leader Yes! Marco is washing up. It's his turn today! Come on, Marco!! Sandy is wearing a purple T-shirt and a cap. She's cooking with that big pan.

THE LOST RUCKSACK

Ranger	Mmm! It smells good! Who's that?
Leader	The boy wearing a yellow jacket? That's Eric. He's going for a walk. That's Tammy over there in the pink swimming costume. She's swimming.
Ranger	Hi! Tammy! Be careful!
Leader	... And her friend, Kathy, look ... she's over there, with the red towel. She's having a shower.
Ranger	Who's that on the pony?
Leader	Oh, that's Ted. Hello, Ted! He's riding.
Ranger	Is that everybody? ... No ... who's that on the tree?
Leader	In the blue T-shirt? That's Conny. She's climbing a rope ... as usual!
Ranger	Well, thanks, Linda. I must go. Have a nice day. Bye!
Kids	Bye!

5   Check the answers asking the children questions e.g. *Who's got a (red towel)? Who's wearing a yellow jacket?* etc.

11 Listen and repeat.

See page 13 of the Introduction for more information on the *Listen and repeat* activities.

1   Focus attention on what each child is doing and tell the children that now they know the children's names, they are going to find out how to talk about the things they are doing.
2   Play the tape and ask the children to listen and then repeat (only the activities), in order to model the sentences.

Tapescript

Look at Paula. She's putting up a tent.
Look at Marco. He's washing up.
Look at Sandy. She's cooking.
Look at Eric. He's going for a walk.
Look at Tammy. She's swimming.
Look at Kathy. She's having a shower.
Look at Ted. He's riding a pony.
Look at Conny. She's climbing a tree.
Look at Ralph. He's making something.
Look at Tony and Anna. They're collecting litter.

3   Explain to the children that you are going to say some sentences describing the camping scene and that they must call out if you are right. If you are wrong they must call out the correct sentence, e.g.
   T *Sandy is cooking.*
   C *That's right!*
   T *Kathy is washing up.*
   C *No! She's having a shower!*
4   Let the children take turns at making the statements.

12 Work in pairs.

1   Prepare the children for this next practice activity by revising the question forms.
2   The children ask and answer questions using the drawing as a prompt, e.g. *What's Marco/he doing? What's Tammy/she doing? What are Anna and Tony/they doing?*

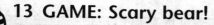

13 GAME: Scary bear!

See page 15 of the Introduction for more suggestions on dealing with games.

1 To play this game, you need the cards used in Activity 7. You need to substitute the sleeping bag, the toilet paper, the knife, the fork and the spoon with the five cards from resource page 140 which were not used in the previous activity. Revise the names of the objects and present the new ones (*bear, bottle, rucksack, rope, horse*).

2 Tell the children that each card is now representing one of the activities listed on the opposite side of the page. To familiarise the children with the written form of the activities, read through each one with the whole class.

3 Explain the rules of the game, then invite one of the children out and model the game for the whole class:

   a in pairs, the children choose one of the names listed on the left-hand side of the book.

   b child A shuffles the cards and places them face down on the desk.

   c child B must choose a card and produce a sentence using one of the activities listed in the book which goes with that card (e.g. *soap – having a shower*). If the sentence is correct, he/she earns points as follows:
   first card: 2 points; second card: 4 points; third card: 6 points; fourth card: 8 points, etc.

   d child B will continue to play until the bear appears. When this happens, he/she counts his/her points and writes them on the book next to the chosen name. Then the children swap over.

4 Model the game for the class with a child, to clarify the rules and highlight the language that can be used.

   B *(I'm) Anna. I'd like this card.*
   A *A tent!*
   B *She's putting up a tent.*
   A *Right.* (Child B marks 2 points next to 'Anna'.)
   B *I'd like this card.*
   A *Scary bear!*
   B *Oh no!*
   A *How many points have you got?*
   B *Two.*
   A *It's my turn.*

14 Mime and write.

1 Call out a child, who chooses an activity to mime. The other children guess what he/she is doing and his/her name is written next to the appropriate card among the ones used in the previous activity.

2 When all the activities have been mimed, the children write the corresponding sentences in their exercise books using the appropriate pronoun, e.g. (Giuseppe and Maria) = *They are putting up a tent.*

15 PROJECT: Take it home!

As a lead-in activity to the project illustrated in the Student's Book, draw the children's attention to the importance of looking after the environment as well as highlighting how discarded packaging can sometimes be used to make amusing toys and objects to play with – like a ship, a pirate, a submarine, a piggy-bank, an egg-timer, etc. from a plastic bottle, or a robot, a pen-holder, a radio, a car from a shoe-box, toilet rolls, etc.

THE LOST RUCKSACK

Lesson 4

OBJECTIVES:	to learn about National Parks and Protected Areas; to stimulate environmental awareness
TARGET LANGUAGE:	animals (*fox, dolphin, grizzly bear, whale, deer, lizard, otter, moose, rat*)
RECYCLED LANGUAGE:	*What shall we do? Let's ... go for a walk*, animals (*eagle, shark, wolf*), the countryside, the weather
MATERIALS:	cassette player and cassette 2, photocopies of resource page 142

CULTURE VULTURE: National Parks

Introduction

Linking back to the theme of recycling and the environment in general, tell the children that in order to protect the environment many special areas are being created. These are called Protected Areas and may be National Parks, Wildlife Reserves, Nature Reserves etc. Ask the children if they have ever visited a place like this and if there are Protected Areas in their country. Explain that they are going to listen to some information about Protected Areas in the English-speaking world.

16 Listen and point.

1 Focus attention on the photos, giving the children some time to observe them carefully. Focus attention on the first, Yellowstone Park, and ask if they have ever heard of it. Give them a clue: tell them to think of an animal cartoon character (the cartoon adventures of Yogi Bear are set in this park). Yellowstone Park is in the central Rocky Mountains between the states of Wyoming, Montana, and Idaho. Oceanworld Manly is in eastern Australia, not far from Sydney. The Lake District National Park is in the north-west of England near the border with Scotland. Death Valley is in California, USA. The Denali National Park is in central Alaska in the USA.

2 Tell the children they are going to listen to the tape and learn the names of these places. Once they have heard these names, ask them in which countries they are. Focus attention on the names of the countries under the photos. Tell them to listen out for the information and write the letter corresponding to the country in the appropriate box. The two, three or four adjacent boxes will be used for the next activity.

Tapescript

Let's look at five National Parks. The first is Yellowstone Park. There are mountains, forests, rivers and waterfalls.
The second one is called Oceanworld Manly and is a Marine Park in the Pacific Ocean.
The third photo shows a beautiful National Park; it's the Lake District National Park. There are many lakes and forests, and it rains a lot!

The fourth photo shows The Death Valley National Park where it is very hot and dry. It's one of the hottest places in the world!
The last photo shows Denali National Park. It snows a lot here and it is very cold.

Where are these parks? Yellowstone is very big, and is in the south-west of the USA. Oceanworld Manly is by the sea in the south-east of Australia. The Lake District National Park is in Cumbria, in the north-west of England. Death Valley is in California in the west of the USA, and Denali National Park is in Alaska, which is in the north-west of the USA.

17 Listen and match.

1   This activity focuses on some of the animals that live in these parks. The children listen and repeat the names of the animals and practise them via pair work question and answer or choral drilling.
2   They listen again and, in the spaces provided, write the numbers of the animals mentioned for each park.

Tapescript

Lots of animals live free in National Parks. Look on the right of the page: there are twelve of these animals:
1   a grizzly bear 2 an eagle 3 a whale 4 a deer 5 a fox 6 a lizard 7 a rat 8 a shark
9   an otter 10 a moose 11 a wolf 12 a dolphin

Yellowstone Park has many kinds of animals; for example, there are grizzly bears, eagles and deer.
Oceanworld Manly is a Marine Park where you can see dolphins, whales and sharks.
In the Lake District some of the animals you can find are deer, foxes, otters, and eagles.
Death Valley is very hot and dry, but there are some small animals; for example lizards and rats.
Denali National Park has animals that prefer colder weather: there are moose, wolves and grizzly bears.

18 PROJECT: National Park wall chart

1   The children bring in or research pictures/drawings of animals to be found in a protected area near their town or in their region.
2   They then write a simple description of the location and the wildlife. E.g. *The Parco nazionale dello Stelvio is in the north of Italy near Switzerland. There are high mountains, trees and flowers. It's cold and in winter it snows. You can see many animals: deer, eagles,* etc. (Present other animals if necessary, e.g. *marmot, mountain goat,* etc.)
3   Alternatively the children could work around a map of their own country marking the protected areas/parks with arrows, descriptions and illustrative material.

19 Listen and colour.

The tapescript may look lengthy yet a closer look will reveal that much of the language contained is active language.

1   Tell the children that a Safari Park is a place where the animals are free and the spectators are in cages (cars). *Has anyone ever been to one? What was it like?* etc.
2   Focus attention on the map and, as a warm-up, ask the children to identify as many animals as they can. Tell them you are going to say which animals you would like to see in the Safari Park. They should listen and colour in red only those animals that you would

THE LOST RUCKSACK

like to see. Now read the following: *I like Safari Parks! They're great! Now, let's see ... I want to see the gorillas – they're really big and strong ... and I'd like to see the chimpanzees, like the one in Tarzan. Then ... I don't like camels! they're so smelly* (mime) *pooohhh! But I want to see the elephants and the eagles.*

3   Tell the children they are going to listen to some visitors in the park discussing first where they want to go. They will then listen to the group as they make their way down to their chosen places in the park.

4   Play the tape through once just to familiarise the children with the characters and the context.

Tapescript

Mr. Robbins	Right. Here we are!
Kids	Hurray!
Mr. Robbins	Let's look at the map. ... Mmm ... What shall we do first?
Kids	I want to see the lions/snakes/bears!
Mr. Robbins	Ssshhh! Listen, we've got two hours. We can't see all the animals ... .
Kids	Oh, no! What a pity!
Mr. Robbins	Now, let's see ... . Tell me, what do you want to see, Tommy?
Tommy	I want to see the crocodiles and those enormous lizards and ...
Silvy	Yuuuuk!
Mr. Robbins	And you, Silvy?
Silvy	I'd like to see the black panthers.
David	And I want to see the snakes.
Mr. Robbins	Mmmm. They're in different areas. What shall we do?
Silvy	Well, all right ... let's see your horrible snakes and crocodiles ...
David	... then, let's see the black panthers ...
Mr. Robbins	This is the reptile house. ... Let's go in!
Tommy	Great! Wow! Look at that enormous lizard ... the black and yellow one!
Silvy	Very nice, Tommy! Take it home with you! Ugh!! I hate lizards!
David	Let's go over there ... there are some fantastic alligators and crocodiles!
Tommy	What's the difference?
Mr. Robbins	Alligators are smaller than crocodiles.
Silvy	Wow! That crocodile is longer than a car!
David	Come on! The snakes are over there ...
Mr. Robbins	Look at that snake ... the big one on the tree ... it's an anaconda. It's the biggest and strongest snake in the world. It can eat a crocodile or a cow ...
Tommy	... or Silvy!
Silvy	Shut up, Tommy! Let's go ...
Silvy	What's in here? ... Aaah! spiders!!
Tommy	I like spiders ... they're big ... and black ... and ...
Silvy	What's that on your shoulder?
Tommy	Aaagh! Where?! Stupid!
Silvy	'I like spiders'!!
Mr. Robbins	That's all here ... let's go and see the black panthers now.
David	Dad! ... I'm thirsty!
Tommy	And I'm hungry!
Mr. Robbins	So what shall we do?
David	There's a kiosk opposite the car park ... it's near the panther area ....
Mr. Robbins	OK. Let's go to the kiosk first.
Tommy	I'd like a burger, please, and ... a large Coke ...

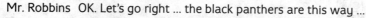

Mr. Robbins	OK. Let's go right … the black panthers are this way …
David	I can't see …. Wait! Look! Near the tree!
Silvy	There are four … they're beautiful! They've got yellow eyes …
Mr. Robbins	Let's go on …
Silvy	Let's turn left here …
Mr. Robbins	We don't want to go back! Let's turn right … and we can see the tigers and lions.
David	Great!
Silvy	Look at that tiger! It's jumping!
Tommy	… and that lion is sleeping …
Mr. Robbins	I'm sorry, but it's five o'clock … it's late; we can't see the bears …
Silvy	Ooh … OK. let's turn left here then …
Tommy	Thanks, Mr. Robbins, that was great fun!

5   Play the tape again up to … *then let's see the black panthers …* . The students should tell you which animals the children would like to see (*lions, snakes, bears, crocodiles, lizards, black panthers*).

6   Tell the children they are now going to listen to the second part of the dialogue in which they have to listen and colour in the circles next to the animals that the visitors have decided to see.

Key

lizards   alligators   crocodiles   snakes   spiders   black panthers   tigers   lions

Extension: a visit to a Safari Park

Using the model dialogue, in pairs the children have short conversations, asking for and giving suggestions as to what they would like to see in the Safari Park. e.g.

A *What shall we do?*

B *I'd like to see (the camels).*

A *OK. Let's go and see the camels./Oh, I don't like camels, let's go and see (the elephants).*

20 Listen and fill in.

1   Hand out copies of resource page 142, which contains the first part of the dialogue from Activity 19.

2   Play the first part of the tapescript from Activity 19.

3   Play the tape again and ask the children to fill in the missing words.

Drama time

6 The Lost Rucksack (see page 10 of the Introduction for notes on Drama time for the story.)

7 DANGER!

Story time

See page 9 of the Introduction for more suggestions on dealing with the story.

1 Remind the children of the story so far. Focus attention on the title *Danger!*, and in L1 ask if anyone knows what this means. Remind the children of where Ben and his friends are, and ask them what *danger* might refer to.

2 Get them to look at the pictures in this episode. Ask the children what they think is taking place. Encourage them to describe in English what they see in the scenes. Where possible, focus on those actions that the children have recently learnt, extending the context, e.g. *What's this? (It's a rope.) Look at Ben. Is he climbing up or down the rope?* Mime *up* and *down*.

3 Make sure that they have understood that:
   a the children can't get out of the cave because the bear is guarding the entrance.
   b they try to gain precious time by feeding the bear biscuits.
   c Jasper discovers a hidden tunnel leading out of the cave, and starts digging.
   d they climb down the tunnel.
   e the bear snatches at the rope and breaks it as Ben is going down, causing him to fall.
   f they find themselves in an underground cavern and they can't get out.
   g the children follow the signal from the transmitter.
   h while looking for new batteries for her torch, Susan discovers that the batteries contain mercury. The children now have all the materials again.
   i they approach the next cave opening, and suddenly their happy expressions fade.

4 Follow the *Story time* procedure on page 9 of the Introduction. Play the tape and ask the children to follow the story in the book.

5 Play the tape again. This time they must listen out for:
   a who the children think might come and help them *(the park ranger)*.
   b what Susan says when she looks at the batteries *(Mercury! The batteries contain mercury!)*
   c what the children hear in the last scene of the episode. (Accept all answers for now).

Lesson 1

OBJECTIVES:	to ask for things; to ask for clarification
TARGET LANGUAGE:	equipment (*calculator, mirror, binoculars, compass, periscope, magnet*), *Can you give me … ? Which ones? The (red) ones.*
RECYCLED LANGUAGE:	colours, shapes, size
MATERIALS:	cassette recorder, cassette 2, photocopies of resource page 137

Introduction

Remind the children of what happened in the story with the rucksacks. *(Ben picked up the wrong rucksack.)* Collect three or four of their schoolbags and put them on your desk. Invite comments about them, e.g. colours, size, etc. Help them with any vocabulary they might need, e.g. *dirty/clean/old/new/heavy*. Keep the rucksacks/schoolbags on your desk for the moment.

1 Listen and repeat. Listen and tick.

See page 13 of the Introduction for the *Listen and repeat* activities.

1 Focus attention on the first picture and ask about the rucksacks in it, e.g. *How many are there? What colour are they? Is this Ben's/Susan's?*

2 Play the tape and ask the children to listen and repeat the dialogue.

3 Ask why Ben didn't give Susan the rucksack immediately. *(He didn't know which one she wanted.)* Ask how Ben asked her about this *(Which one?)* and how she answered *(The red one).*

4 Get the children to repeat the dialogue. Drill the sentences using choral and group drilling.

5 Dramatise the scene using the children's bags on your desk so that they ask you *Can you give me my rucksack, please?* Ask *Which one?* and they answer, e.g. *The black one.* You can also use classroom objects to illustrate how *one* is used, e.g. *pencil: the long one/the short one, rubber: the big one/the small one,* etc.

6 Focus attention on the numbered objects on the page and ask the children what they notice about the drawings. (The same object is presented twice, but there is a distinguishing feature in each.) Check that the children have recognised what each object is. Tell them they are going to learn the names of these objects. Play the tape, then ask the children to listen and repeat.

Tapescript

Look at these objects in the shop windows. Here are the names:
1 calculator 2 mirror 3 binoculars 4 compass 5 periscope 6 magnet

7 Set the scene for the next dialogue. Explain that Ben, Susan and Toby have to decide which one they want to buy. Elicit the differences between each pair of objects, then play the tape. The children listen and tick the chosen object.

Tapescript

Now listen. Toby, Ben and Susan are in the shop.

One

Toby	Can you give me that calculator, please?
Shop Assistant	Which one?
Toby	The black one.

Two

Ben	Can you give me that mirror, please?
Shop Assistant	Which one?
Ben	The round one.

Three

Susan	Can you give me those binoculars, please?
Shop Assistant	Which ones?
Susan	The new ones.

Four

Toby	Can you give me that compass, please?
Shop Assistant	Which one?
Toby	The big one.

Five

Ben	Can you give me that periscope, please?
Shop Assistant	Which one?
Ben	The American one.

DANGER!

Six

Susan	Can you give me that magnet, please?
Shop Assistant	Which one?
Susan	The green and blue one.

8   In the third dialogue the plural example has been introduced especially to provide scope for extension should you so wish. If not, no focus need to be made.

2   Read and match.

1   Focus attention on the written forms and explain that they have to be linked to objects illustrated in Activity 1.
2   Individually, they read and match, writing the corresponding number in the box provided.

Extension: Play shop!

To extend the above language to include *Thank you, How much is it? Here you are,* the children could enact short scenes from shops using empty packaging, drawings, school objects, clothes, etc. for the products. For money use copies of resource page 137.

3   Ask and answer.

1   Collect a selection of the classroom items used in previous practice exercises. Put them all on your desk, and get the children to claim their belongings using the dialogues above as a model.
2   Model the dialogue first with one child, then let another child take your place.
3   Let the children work in pairs.

Lesson 2

OBJECTIVES:	to describe objects; to give explanations with *because;* to develop listening skills
TARGET LANGUAGE:	*Which one do you want?*
RECYCLED LANGUAGE:	*I like (this one) because ... / It's got ... / There is/are ... .*
MATERIALS:	cassette recorder, cassette 2

Introduction

Tell the children to imagine that they could design their own rucksacks. Ask them what 'optionals' they would include.

4   Listen and mark B, T or S.

1   Focus attention on the three rucksacks and explain that Doctor Alpha has just finished them.
2   Give the children time to examine them carefully and encourage them to talk about them, e.g. *The orange one has got a mirror. There's an umbrella on the red one. I like the blue one. Why? Because it's got a cassette player,* etc.

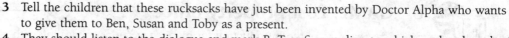

3 Tell the children that these rucksacks have just been invented by Doctor Alpha who wants to give them to Ben, Susan and Toby as a present.

4 They should listen to the dialogue and mark B, T or S according to which rucksack each of the children chooses. The third dialogue has been included for consolidation purposes – clearly once they have identified the owners of the first two, there is only one bag left! N.B. Not all the features of the three rucksacks are mentioned on the tape; during a second or third listening, ask the children which objects are not mentioned. Ask *Which one is your favourite? Why?*

Tapescript

Doctor Alpha	... Right ... now this one ...
Ben	Hello, Dad! Wow! What are you doing?
Doctor Alpha	I'm working on these new rucksacks ... there!
Susan	Wow! They're fantastic!
Doctor Alpha	Yes ... they're very special ... and they're for you!
Toby	For us? Wow! Thank you!
Doctor Alpha	Now then, Toby, you're the youngest ... which one do you want?
Toby	Well ... they're all brilliant, Doctor Alpha ... but I think I like this one best!
Doctor Alpha	Mmm, why? The colour?
Toby	No, I like it because it's got a map pocket and a camera! And look! Fantastic! ... there's a walkie-talkie, a digital clock, and ... what's this?
Doctor Alpha	Oh, yes, that's a special mirror – it's a very good idea.
Toby	Why?
Doctor Alpha	Because you can see behind you when you're walking!
Toby	Magic! Can I have this one, please?
Doctor Alpha	Of course. Here you are. Now, Ben ... Susan ... what about you?
Ben	I like them both. You can choose, Susan.
Susan	Thanks, Ben. Well, I like this one because it's got a calculator and that's great for my maths homework ... and look! Great! It's got a mini TV and an electronic diary for my messages!
Toby	So she can send messages to Paul Woodcock ...
Susan	Oh! Shut up, Toby! And ... er ... what's this, Doctor Alpha?
Doctor Alpha	It's an umbrella ... there ... clever, eh?
Susan	Can I have this one, please? Is that OK with you, Ben?
Ben	Yes, because I like music, and this one has got a stereo, and there's a place for my CDs.
Doctor Alpha	It's got a periscope, you know!
Ben	What? Where? Why?
Doctor Alpha	Here. It's great, because you can see over walls!
Ben	Mmm. I like this video game ... thanks a lot, Dad.
Doctor Alpha	Good, good, good! Now, I've got a little job for you ...

5 Design a rucksack.

1 Each child invents his/her own accessories to build into his/her rucksack and then draws the finished product.

2 Help them to write the description by putting key language on the board, e.g. *This is my rucksack. It's got a/some... . There's a/There are some ... . I like it because (it's black and white ... like my team! My favourite object is (the walkman) because I like (music),* etc.

DANGER!

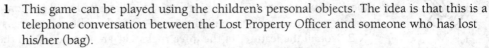

6 GAME: Lost property office

See page 15 of the Introduction for more suggestions on dealing with games.

1 This game can be played using the children's personal objects. The idea is that this is a telephone conversation between the Lost Property Officer and someone who has lost his/her (bag).

2 Explain that the officer, once he/she has identified the (bag), must be certain that it does belong to the person asking for it. To do this he/she asks questions that only the owner can answer.

3 Elicit useful phrases from the children and pre-teach new language items (these items are 'disposable' and only serve to play the game).

4 Collect three or four of the objects and place them on your desk. Place a chair in front of the desk and turn it round so that the child who will sit there has his/her back to the child who will play the Lost Property Officer.

5 Call out one child who will be the Lost Property Officer and one of the owners of the objects on your desk. The officer asks questions to find out which bag belongs to the child.

6 Write up the following mini-dialogue guide for the children to use during the game:

Officer	*Hello, can I help you?*
Customer	*Yes, please. I've lost my (bag).*
Officer	*What colour is it?*
Customer	*It's (red and green).*
Officer	*Is it big or small?*
Customer	*It's (big).*
Officer	*What's in it?*
Customer	*(Three books, a pencil case, a cake.)*
Officer	*Is there an exercise book?*
Customer	*No, there isn't.*
Officer	*(When satisfied) Yes, OK. I've got your (bag) here!*
Customer	*Thank you.*

Lesson 3

OBJECTIVES:	to identify jobs; to describe what people do in their jobs
TARGET LANGUAGE:	*What's his/her job? He's /She's a... , jobs (pilot, bus driver, chemist, shop assistant, clerk, policeman, ticket inspector, park ranger), Present Simple tense (s/he drives, checks, sells), outside/ inside, during the day/at night, van*
RECYCLED LANGUAGE:	*jeep, car*
PREVIEW:	*sometimes*
MATERIALS:	cassette recorder, cassette 2

Introduction

1 Introduce the theme of work and jobs by asking the children what they would like to do when they grow up and why.

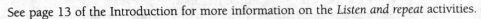

2 Ask the children about one or two well-known jobs, e.g. *policeman/woman, bus driver, pilot,* etc. and discuss what each job involves.
3 Tell the class that in the story so far, Ben and his friends have met several people doing their jobs: *an information clerk at the airport, a chemist, a shop assistant, a travel agent, a policeman, a railway guard.*
4 Ask what they would like about these jobs, and what aspects they might not find so enjoyable.

7 Listen and repeat.

See page 13 of the Introduction for more information on the *Listen and repeat* activities.

1 Focus attention on the drawing on top of page 58 and invite suggestions as to what the person's job may be. Focus attention on the shelves and counter.
2 Read the introductory text and clarify where necessary. Explain *work* and *sell.* Tell the children they are going to learn how to ask and answer about people's jobs. Remind the children of the difference between *his* and *her.*
3 Play the tape and ask the children to listen.
4 Play the tape again. Drill the dialogue using choral and group drilling.
5 Now focus attention on the eight drawings showing other jobs and ask the children if they remember any of them from the storyline. (*the chemist, shop assistant, travel agency clerk, policeman* and *ticket inspector* have appeared briefly in the story.)
6 Present, model and drill the jobs in the same way highlighted in points 3 and 4.

Tapescript

1 **What's his job?**
   He's a pilot.
2 **What's his job?**
   He's a bus driver.
3 **What's her job?**
   She's a chemist.
4 **What's his job?**
   He's a shop assistant.
5 **What's her job?**
   She's a clerk.
6 **What's his job?**
   He's a policeman.
7 **What's his job?**
   He's a ticket inspector.
8 **What's his job?**
   He's a park ranger.

7 The children practise in pairs, pointing to a drawing and asking *What's his/her job? He's/She's a (shop assistant).*

8 Listen and match.

1 Tell the children they are going to listen to the people from Activity 7 saying a phrase they often use at work.
2 The children listen to the tape twice; the first time they listen and identify the speech bubbles, the second time they listen and match the speech bubbles to the jobs.
3 The children first check in pairs pointing to the speech bubbles in turn and giving their opinion saying *I think this is the (pilot).*
4 Check with the class asking *Who says 'Tickets please!'?*

Tapescript and key
Tickets, please! (7)
Here's your medicine, madam. (3)
Can I help you? (4)
Stop! (6)
The camping area is over there. (8)
Good morning, and welcome to Kennedy Airport. (1)
Next stop, Liverpool Street. (2)
Where do you want to go? (5)

DANGER!

9 Listen and repeat.

See page 13 of the Introduction for more information on the *Listen and repeat* activities.

1 Ask the children to read the leader text to say what they think a typical day is like for a park ranger.
2 While the children are offering suggestions, take the opportunity to preview relevant items, e.g. if the children mention the fact that rangers wear a uniform, say in English *Oh, yes, a uniform!* and accompany the utterance with mime.
3 Focus attention on the pictures and give the children a moment to study them. Ask them what they understand from the drawings.
4 Play the tape. The children point to the corresponding pictures.
5 They listen a second time and repeat.
6 The third time they listen and repeat again. Stop the tape after each three pictures to allow them time to assimilate the information.

i **LISTEN AND REPEAT SECTIONS: with more complex listen and repeat activities it is useful to break the listening into sections, constantly recapping the previous section as you progress.**

7 Say a sentence and get them to point to the appropriate drawing. In pairs, they do the same.

10 Listen and tick. Describe.

1 Focus attention on the grid and elicit what the visual prompts next to the verbs indicate: *uniform, inside, outside, during the day, at night, a plane, a car, a bus, a jeep, the park, tickets, documents, toys, medicines, around the park, around the world, around the town.*
2 Present, model and drill the new items, e.g. *documents*.
3 Ask why the items have been grouped in the way shown, i.e. the picture illustrates a possible substitution using the same verb, e.g. *sells medicines/toys*.
4 Tell the children you are going to mime a moment in the park ranger's day and they have to guess which it is. Give them a prompt (spoken or visual), e.g. *jeep*, to which they respond *He drives a jeep*.
5 Focus attention on the bus driver. Tell them you are going to give them some information about his job and they should tell you if each sentence is true or false. This will give you the opportunity to elicit substitute items, e.g.
    T *He drives a jeep.*
    C *False!*
    T (accompanying with mime) *Right! He doesn't drive a jeep. A car? Does he drive a car?*
    C *No!*
    T *What does he drive?*
    C *He drives a bus.*

i **RELEVANT INFORMATION: before doing the activity clarify that the activities described must be pertinent to the person's job and not with, say, getting to work or social activities, e.g. a shop assistant drives a car but this is not part of his job. Clarify that in English *work outside* refers to working in the open air like, say, a builder.**

6 Explain that the children are going to listen to some short descriptions of three jobs: the chemist, the ticket inspector and the shop assistant, and that they will have to put a tick in the box corresponding to what they hear.
7 Do the description of the park ranger's work together by way of example, letting them

listen again to the recorded description of his work in Activity 9, or by reading out the tapescript.

8   The children listen to the job descriptions and put a tick in the appropriate boxes. (NB. Obviously, not all the boxes are marked.)

Tapescript

This is Alice. She's a chemist. She wears a uniform. She works inside. She works during the day. Sometimes she works at night. She sells medicines.
This is George. He's a ticket inspector. He wears a uniform. He works during the day. Sometimes he works at night. He checks tickets.
This is Alex. He's a shop assistant. He works inside. He works during the day. He sells toys.

9   In pairs, each child chooses two of the remaining four jobs and fills in the ticks. He/she then describes the job to his/her partner who listens and marks the boxes accordingly. They then swap over. If they don't agree they may discuss the matter. Sometimes the information does not fit all the cases exactly. In this case the boxes are best left unticked.

Extension: writing task

The children choose one or more of the jobs and using the information in the grid they write a short description of the job. Model the activity first, choosing one of the jobs, eliciting how they would describe it and writing the description on the board. Choose another job and go through the example on the board highlighting the substitutions.

11 Draw and describe.

1   Ask the children about their parents' jobs. Do they do any of these jobs? Supply new vocabulary to enable them to say what the members of their family do. Model and drill it.
2   The children draw their parents and describe the jobs they do.

Lesson 4

OBJECTIVES:	to ask about jobs; to describe what people do in their jobs
TARGET LANGUAGE:	*Does he/she ...? Yes, he/she does. No, he/she doesn't.*
RECYCLED LANGUAGE:	jobs
PREVIEW:	*through, never*
MATERIALS:	cassette recorder, cassette 2, photocopies of resource page 143

Introduction

Remind the children of the story when Ben, Susan and Toby discovered they couldn't get out of the cave because of the bear. How did they think help might arrive? (*The park ranger.*) Why? (*Because he checks the park every day.*) Why wouldn't he find the children? (*Because he doesn't check the caves.*)

DANGER!

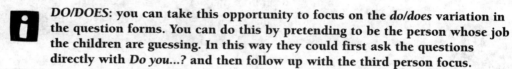

12 Listen and repeat.

See page 13 of the Introduction for the *Listen and repeat* activities.

1. Focus attention on the presentation flash, and clarify that Susan and Toby are both thinking of the park ranger. Tell the children that they are going to listen to how Susan and Toby asked Ben about what the ranger does every day.
2. Play the tape and ask the children to listen and repeat.
3. Play the tape again. Model the dialogue using choral and group drilling.
4. Using the previous page, use the ranger's activities to practise the short answer forms *Yes, he does/No, he doesn't* by asking the children questions, e.g. *Does he drive a motorbike? (No, he doesn't.) Does he work outside? (Yes, he does.)* etc.
5. Extend the practice to the other jobs dealt with by using the grid in Activity 10.

13 Guess the job.

1. In the previous activity the children learnt how to respond *Yes* or *No*. Now ask them to look at the grid and ask you a question about, say, the pilot.
2. When they are confident, tell them they are going to play a guessing game: you think of a job and they have to guess it by asking you questions but you may only answer *Yes* or *No*.
3. Model the game and then let the children play it in pairs.

> **ⓘ** **DO/DOES: you can take this opportunity to focus on the *do/does* variation in the question forms. You can do this by pretending to be the person whose job the children are guessing. In this way they could first ask the questions directly with *Do you...?* and then follow up with the third person focus.**

14 Listen and point. Read and answer.

1. Focus attention on the artwork and explain that these are scenes from someone's typical working day. Elicit from the children whose job is being described *(a stunt-woman)*.
2. Tell the children they are going to listen to a description of Danji's typical day. They follow by pointing to the picture that corresponds to the description. The vocabulary is not completely unfamiliar yet is presented in a slightly different context. E.g. *goes* and *gym* have been dealt with but not *goes to the gym*. Explain that *work* can be both a verb and a noun.
3. The children listen to the tape and point to the appropriate pictures. Model and drill the new items describing activities.
4. The children read the text and answer the questions with either *Yes, she does* or *No, she doesn't*. Explain that they must only take the information from the text!

15 SONG: Stunt lady

See page 15 of the Introduction for more information on dealing with songs and raps.

1. Hand out copies of resource page 143 and focus attention on the illustrations. Ask the children what they think is happening.
2. Let them read the words to the song, and match the pictures to the relevant descriptions.
3. Teach them the song in the usual way, starting with a reading-out-loud phase to set the rhythm. When they are confident with the words, let them try singing.
4. The children could also mime what the intrepid Danji is doing during her stunts.

Drama time

7 Danger! (See page 10 of the Introduction for notes on *Drama time* for the story.)

8 REVISION

Lesson 1

> OBJECTIVES: to revise the language presented in Units 5–7
> MATERIALS: cassette player, cassette 2, dice, counters, photocopies of resource pages 144–145

1 Look and find.

1 Hand out copies of resource page 144.
2 Focus attention on the numbered items and explain that they have to decide what each item is and then find the corresponding word in the box to the right of the scene. The words may run vertically or horizontally.
3 When they find a word it is better if they outline it in order to see which areas of the puzzle are still 'unexplored'. Once a word has been found, e.g. *wolf*, the children cross off the number 1 (as in the example) in the appropriate place.
4 The activity may be done individually or in pairs.

2 The sentence snake.

1 Hand out copies of resource page 145. The sentence snake is a game board in the shape of a coil divided into 24 sections. Each section contains the first half or the second half of 12 sentences, which the children must match together correctly.
2 This activity is played in two stages. The first stage involves the children playing in pairs, one against the other, each winning as many phrases as possible. In the second stage the two children pool their phrases and build a dialogue which is then fitted to the scenes in the drawings below.
3 In stage one, each child in turn throws a dice and moves his/her counter along the coiled sentence snake according to the number thrown on the dice. When he/she lands on a section he finds the other half of the phrase and colours both halves. When all the phrases have been taken the player with more phrases has won.

 ALTERNATIVE MARKING: each player may put his/her 'mark' – a piece of coloured paper, another counter, a small sweet, etc. – on the sections to show they have been taken. This will enable the children to re-use the game, with other partners or at other times.

4 In stage two the children look at the dialogue scenes and speech bubbles under the sentence snake. They cut out the speech bubbles, write the appropriate phrase and stick them next to the appropriate speaker. This will also serve as a checking phase for the previous stage of the game.

Key

1 Good morning. Good morning.	2 Can I help you?	3 I'd like that pullover please.
4 Which one?	5 The red one.	6 Here you are.
7 How much is it?	8 £40. (40 pounds.)	9 Here you are.
10 Thank you.	11 Good-bye!	

REVISION

Lesson 2

OBJECTIVES:
MATERIALS:

to revise the language presented in Units 5–7
cassette player, cassette 2, photocopies of resource
page 146, dice, counters

3 GAME: Job Cluedo

See page 15 of the Introduction for more suggestions on dealing with games.

1 This game involves the use of a minimum of eight job cards from resource page 146. Each job card contains a drawing of the job plus three clues. For example, the drawing of policeman includes these sentences:
1 He wears a uniform. 2 He drives a car. 3 He checks documents.

> **DIFFICULTY OF CLUES: the clues are organised so that the first leaves scope for guessing, the second reduces the choice and the third practically gives it away!**

2 The board game in the Student's Book consists of 30 squares each containing a drawing of an object or of someone involved in an activity or of a prompt word.

3 Explain the rules of the game, which are as follows:
  a the children play in groups of four. Each takes a job card, looks at it without saying anything and places it face down on the board in the space provided at the four corners. Each player 'looks after' one of these cards. The information on it must remain secret.
  b the objective of the game is to discover two of the mystery jobs (clearly not the one they have already seen). To do this, the first player throws the dice and moves his/her counter according to the number thrown. Before starting the game, the children have to decide which box they have to start from, and then they move clockwise.
  c he/she performs the language task required by the square he/she has landed on:
     1 for squares containing an object, animal or shop the player has to say the name, e.g. *It's a shark!*
     2 for squares containing people doing something the player has to say what the character is doing, e.g. *He's putting up a tent.*
     3 for squares containing words the player has to say a sentence containing that word, e.g. *What shall we do?*
  d if correct, the player collects a point. When a player has three points, he/she may choose a card (again, not his/her own!) and ask the 'keeper' for the first clue.
  e the 'keeper' whispers the clue to the player without the others hearing.

> **ALTERNATIVE CLUES: a) he/she writes the clue down on a slip of paper and hands it to the player or b) shows the relevant sentence to the player covering the drawing and the other clues.**

  f when a player has a clue, he/she may either guess the job or wait for another clue. If the player decides to guess, he/she declares *I know!* and whispers the name of the job to the keeper. If the guess is correct, he/she has won one job and continues playing for the second. If the guess is incorrect, the player must continue playing but must choose another mystery job card.

g the first player to get two jobs correct is the winner.

EXTRA CARDS: the cards may be supplemented with extra jobs/clues at the teacher's discretion. The children can be involved in the producing of the playing cards by using the blank cards available on resource page 146.

Storyboard

See page 11 of the Introduction for notes on the *Storyboard*.

Divide the class into small groups. Get each group to draw the principal scenes from the story in Units 5, 6 and 7. This session of the *Storyboard* will continue the wall frieze. See the notes in Unit 4 Lesson 2 page 50 for details of how to handle the session.

9 THE PRINCE OF ARION

Story time

See page 9 of the Introduction for more suggestions on dealing with the story.

1 Remind the children of the story so far. Ask if they remember how the last episode of the story finished. (The children had heard a strange sound as they approached the next cave.) Invite suggestions as to what this noise could be.

2 Focus attention on the title *The Prince of Arion*, and in L1 ask if anyone knows what this means.

3 Remind the children of where Ben and his friends are and how they got there. Ask what their problem is now. (The children are trapped in the underground caves.) Ask how they think they might escape from the caves. Accept all answers for the moment.

4 Get them to look at the pictures in this episode. Ask the children what they think is taking place. Encourage them to describe what they see in the scenes in English. Where possible focus on those items that the children have recently learnt. Make sure that they all understand that:

a the children have disturbed a colony of bats, and they are frightened of bats.

b to follow the signal from the transmitter they must pass through the bats' cave.

c the rucksack which Ben took by accident contains a first-aid kit (with alcohol), a flag and some matches.

d Ben has the idea of making a torch from these things to keep the bats away.

e the transmitter signal is getting stronger all the time.

f Ben remembers the code to open the capsule. It is the date (day and month) of Halloween.

g Kanda realises that the children have come to help him.

h the water level is rising rapidly and the children are in danger.

i Kanda tells them to get into the capsule, which gently rises out of the water.

j while they are heading upwards into the sky Jasper accidentally presses a button.

k Jasper has switched off the automatic pilot and the capsule is momentarily out of control heading for a funfair.

5 Follow the *Story time* procedure on page 9 of the Introduction. Play the tape and ask the children to follow the story on the book.

6 Play the tape again. This time they have to listen out for:

a what Susan says about the bats (*I don't like bats!*).

b what date Ben mentions and why (*Halloween … 31st October! Yes! 31? …10? The date is the code to open the capsule*).

c what two questions Toby and Susan ask Ben about Kanda (*Does he understand English? Does he know we are friends?*)

d what instructions Toby gives Kanda as they fly out of the tunnel (*Turn left! Turn right!*).

To help the children find the answers to these questions, stop the tape just before the relevant section of the dialogue.

Lesson 1

OBJECTIVES:	to say what you are afraid of and why; to agree
TARGET LANGUAGE:	*I'm afraid of …, the dark, water, spiders, mice, bees, dirty, hairy, slimy, fly, sting, bite*
RECYCLED LANGUAGE:	*Why? Because they're … ., Me too!*
MATERIALS:	cassette recorder, cassette 2, photocopies of resource page 147

Introduction

1 Ask the children what sort of things they are frightened of and why. Ask what sort of things they could do to try and get over their fears.

2 Remind them of the story and ask what Ben and his friends were afraid of (bats). Using mime and suitable facial expressions say *Uuuughh! I'm afraid of bats!* Make this a humorous gesture to reassure the children.

1 Listen and repeat.

See page 13 of the Introduction for more information on the *Listen and repeat* activities.

1 Focus attention on the flashback scene and ask the children if they remember what Ben says to Susan. Ask them if they think Susan is afraid of bats and what makes them think so.

2 Play the tape and ask the children to listen and repeat. Model and drill the dialogue.

3 Explain that they are now going to learn the names of other things that some people are frightened of. Focus attention on the six scenes below the presentation flash. Give the children time to identify the frightening element in each scene (*snakes, the dark, water, spiders, mice, dogs, bees*).

4 To deal with this section use the same procedure highlighted in point 2.

Tapescript

1 I'm afraid of snakes.   2 I'm afraid of the dark.   3 I'm afraid of water.
4 I'm afraid of spiders.   5 I'm afraid of mice.   6 I'm afraid of dogs.
7 I'm afraid of bees.

5 Explain that when they agree or disagree with the speaker they can say *Me too!* or *I'm not!*

> **AGREEING/DISAGREEING: for the purposes of this and successive activities it might be useful to introduce here *I'm not!* as a way of disagreeing with the speaker. If you choose to do this, focus attention on the stress on *I'm not!***

6 During a second listening get the children to put up their hands if they agree with what the speaker says and shout *Me too!*

7 In pairs, one child says the things he/she is afraid of and child B responds, agreeing or disagreeing with the statement, e.g.
A *I'm afraid of (the dark).*
B *Me too!*
B *I'm afraid of (dogs).*
A *I'm not!*

2 Listen and tick.

1 Tell the children they are going to listen to some people speaking about their fears. Focus attention on the grid, and go through the names of the children so that the class will recognise them during the listening phase.

2 Explain that they have to listen and tick the appropriate box.

Tapescript

Adult   This book is for you, Kim. It's about spiders.
Kim   Yuuughh! No thank you! I'm afraid of spiders!
Adult   Really?
Kim   Yes, I'm afraid of spiders, snakes ... yuuuk! ... and bees.
Adult   Bees? Why are you afraid of bees?

THE PRINCE OF ARION

Kim	Because they sting! Zzzickk!!
Adult	What about you, Silvy?
Silvy	Oh, I'm not afraid of bees, but I'm afraid of mice.
Adult	Why?
Silvy	I don't know ... I think it's because they're dirty.
Adult	Mmm, I see.
Marvin	I've got a mouse called Tippy – he's really nice!
Adult	What are you afraid of, Marvin?
Marvin	Nothing ...
Kim	What about snakes, Marvin?
Marvin	Well ... yes, I'm afraid of snakes ... because they're long and slimy ...
Lindy	Snakes aren't slimy ... they're dry! Are you afraid of dogs, Marvin?
Marvin	Eer... no ... wait a minute, I know! I'm afraid of water!
All	Water? Why?
Marvin	Because I can't swim!
Adult	What about you, Lindy?
Lindy	I'm not afraid of water, but I'm afraid of dogs ...
Silvy	Big ones or small ones?
Lindy	Errr ... big ones because they bite! ... And I'm always afraid of the dark ...
Kim	Me too!
Silvy	Me too!
Marvin	Me too!
Adult	Why?
Lindy	Because I always think there's something in the cupboard!
Kim	Yes ... or behind the door!
Silvy	... or under the bed ...
Marvin	... or in the bed!

3   When the children have finished, check the activity by inviting them to tell you what the four children are afraid of, e.g.
   T *Kim?*   **C** *He's afraid of bees!*

3 Listen and choose.

1   Let the children observe the multiple choice statements on the page. Give them a few minutes to study them carefully.
2   Read through the multiple choice answers with the class and explain that in the dialogue they have just heard, the four children gave a reason for their fears. Explain that only one of the answers is correct.
3   Help the children with any comprehension problems.
4   The children listen to the dialogue for Activity 2 again and mark the correct reason by underlining the correct alternative.

4 Ask and answer.

1   Reproduce on the board the grid in Activity 2.
2   As a mingling activity, the children must find one child in the class who is afraid of each object. Alternatively the children interview three or four classmates about their fears, asking *What are you afraid of?* and *Are you afraid of ... ?*
3   Check that they can explain their reasons, and supply vocabulary where necessary.
4   Then they draw the object of their fear in the box provided and complete the sentence.

5 SONG: Spider

See page 15 of the Introduction for more information on dealing with songs and raps.

1 Hand out copies of resource page 147. This simple song recycles the target structure in this lesson and provides an optional miming activity to accompany the song.
2 The first two verses are provided. Teach them these in the usual way. Then the children can make up their own verses by substituting the 'scary' animal.

Extension: mime and guess!

After singing the two ready-made verses, the children do a team mime of one or some of the scary things. One team sings the line but substitutes the scary item of their choice by miming it. If classroom space permits, as soon as the miming team has sung the line *Touch one if you can!*, the guessing team can try and touch/catch one of them (the scary animal) before they reach a safe base. Alternatively they simply call out the name of the animal/item.

Lesson 2

OBJECTIVES:	to find out about and describe animal habits
TARGET LANGUAGE:	*Does it ... ? / Is it ...?*
RECYCLED LANGUAGE:	*Can ...? / Have you got ...?*, short answer forms
MATERIALS:	cassette recorder, cassette 2, photocopies of resource page 148

Introduction

1 Remind the children of the bat attack in the story. Ask them if they know anything about bats, e.g. *Are they big? Can they see? Can you see them during the day? Are they strong? Where do they live?*
2 Tell them that they are going to discover some interesting facts about some rather particular kinds of animals.
3 Focus attention on the page. Explain that it shows photos of impressive animals from different parts of the world.

6 Listen and answer.

1 Focus attention on the photo of the vampire bat.
2 Read through the questions with the class. Explain the meaning of *blood* and *poisonous*.
3 Encourage the children to give their opinions about this creature. Accept all answers for the moment.
4 Tell the children they are going to listen to a description of the animal and they should listen and afterwards try to answer the questions. Tell the children that not all the pieces of information are in the same order as the questions.
5 Listen to the tape several times taking two questions at a time.
6 Check with the whole class.

THE PRINCE OF ARION

Tapescript
There are many types of bats in the world, but this is the strangest ... it's a vampire bat. The vampire bat lives in South America. It is not very big and it's not poisonous, but it is dangerous because it sometimes attacks man. Some bats eat insects but the vampire bat eats blood!

7 Read, ask and mark M, BW or A.

1 Focus attention on the photos and read the names of the animals. Ask the children questions about what they see, e.g. *Is this bat bigger/smaller than the vampire bat? What colour is the spider? It's got a red mark; do you think it is dangerous? Do you think it lives in (your country)? Do you think it's (slimy/hairy/dirty/)? etc.*

2 Photocopy resource page 148 and cut up the descriptions.

3 Divide the class in groups of three and give each child in the group one of the descriptions.

4 The children must discover the information they need to fill in the grid in their books by asking questions to the other two in the group.

5 Before starting the activity, model and drill the questions they could use:
   A *Have you got (the anaconda)?*
   B *Yes, I have.*
   A *Does it live in (Java)?*
   B *No, it doesn't. It lives in (South America).*
   etc.

6 After they have completed the grid, check with the class and ask what information they had which was not requested by the others in their group.

8 Choose and write.

1 The children write a simple description of one of the animals.
2 Model the activity on the board first.

Lesson 3

OBJECTIVES:	to describe routines and habits; to express degrees of frequency
TARGET LANGUAGE:	present simple tense (s/*he uses, wears, takes, looks after, finds*), *always, often, sometimes, never*
RECYCLED LANGUAGE:	present simple tense (*want, live, get up, go, see, use, wear*), *compass, camera, computer, hat, message*
MATERIALS:	cassette recorder, cassette 2

Introduction

Remind the children of what happened when Ben and his friends were trying to remember the code to open the space capsule. Ask them who remembered the code (*Ben*). Ask if Toby remembered the code. *Why not? What was the problem?* (*Toby never remembers numbers.*) Can they remember what the code was? (*Halloween: 31 – 10*)

9 Listen and repeat.

See page 13 of the Introduction for more information on the *Listen and repeat* activities.

1 Focus attention on the first flashback showing Toby. Ask if Toby has a good memory for numbers and focus attention on *never*. Accompany this with mime to emphasise the impact of *never*. The children listen and repeat.

2 Focus attention on the second flashback and ask the children *Where's the capsule going?* (*Back to the spaceship.*) Ask them how they know. (*Because it always goes back to the spaceship.*)

3 The children listen and repeat.

4 Tell the children they are going to learn how to talk about how often things happen, and introduce the other adverbs of frequency *often* and *sometimes*. (The children should be able to recognise the latter as they have already met it in Unit 7.)

5 Focus attention on the calendar diagram as an illustration of the different degrees of frequency. Play the tape and ask the children to repeat the adverbs. Model and drill them one at a time.

Tapescript

always often sometimes never

6 Let the children practise the frequency adverbs. For example:
   T *Do you have (Maths) on (Tuesday)?*
   C *Yes, always./No, never.*
   T (ask the children to repeat this model sentence) *I always/never have (Maths) on (Tuesday).*

7 You can suggest other dialogues by following the above example.

10 Listen and read. Read and answer.

1 Focus attention on the description of Professor Storm. Ask the children questions about the picture, e.g. *Where is he? What's this? What can you see behind Professor Storm?* etc.

2 Tell them they are going to listen to a recording of the description. They must follow it in their books. Explain that some words are missing. On the tape, these words are preceded by a sound and a pause (*). They have to try and guess the words before they hear them.

Tapescript and Key

This is Professor Storm. He's a zoologist and he lives in a small house in Africa. He (*) *always* gets up early and goes into the jungle to study animals. He finds the right place to hide and he (*) *never* makes a noise because he doesn't want to disturb the animals. He (*) *often* finds young animals who need help. He (*) *sometimes* takes them home and looks after them for a few months. In this photo he is with Mira, a baby monkey without a mother ... .

3 Check with the class that they have answered correctly.

4 Write the following comprehension questions on the board. The children then copy them into their exercise books and answer them. Where possible the children should answer using one of the target items *always, often, sometimes* or *never*. However, accept *Yes, he does/No, he doesn't* as alternative answers.
   1 What's Professor Storm's job? (Zoologist)
   2 Where does he live? (In Africa/In a small house)
   3 When does he get up early? (Always/He always gets up early.)
   4 Does he make a noise when he's in the jungle? (Never/He never makes a noise.)
   5 Why? (Because he doesn't want to disturb the animals.)
   6 Does he find young animals in the jungle? (Often/He often finds young animals.)
   7 Does he take them home? (Sometimes/He sometimes takes them home.)

THE PRINCE OF ARION

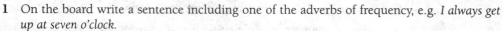

11 Look and write.

1 On the board write a sentence including one of the adverbs of frequency, e.g. *I always get up at seven o'clock.*
2 Tell the children to look at the four diagrams in Activity 9 and tell them that you are going to use one of these rows of lights in place of one of the words in the sentence. Elicit which word you are going to take out (*always*) and which row of lights you are going to substitute it with (the four red dots).
3 Focus attention on the sentences in Activity 11 and explain that these also contain diagrams and small pictures in place of words. Get them to look at the first sentence which has been done by way of example.
4 The children have to decode the illustrated sentences and write the completed sentences in their exercise books.

Key

1 He often uses a compass. 2 He always wears a hat. 3 He never goes into the jungle at night.
4 He always takes a rucksack with binoculars and a computer in it.
5 He sometimes sees crocodiles and he often sees snakes.
6 He sometimes takes photos/a camera. 7 He often uses a radio to send messages.

12 Listen and colour.

1 Tell the children that Professor Storm sends regular reports to his Research Centre so that Mira's progress can be monitored.
2 Let them observe the scenes in the four different messages. Ask the children *What's she doing? Where is she? Look at scene 4: is Mira bigger or smaller than in scene 2?* etc.
3 Focus attention on the scenes where Mira is swinging from the lamp and teasing the cat and introduce *swings* and *teases*.
4 Focus attention on the circles under each picture and ask the children why they are there. They have to listen to the tape and indicate the frequency with which Mira does certain things. They show this by colouring in the appropriate number of circles (as shown in previous activities).
5 The first time, the children listen to the whole script following the scenes.
6 The second time, stop the tape so as to allow them time to colour in the circles.

Tapescript

Message One
Professor Hello, it's Professor Storm. Here's my report on Mira the monkey. Everything's fine, she's very small, she sometimes gets out of her basket and she always stays in the house. She always drinks her morning milk. She's a wonderful little monkey!

Message Two
Hello ... er ... it's Professor Storm with my second report on Mira, the monkey. She's bigger now and stronger. She sometimes eats bananas and ... she often makes a noise. She never stays in her basket and she sometimes plays with the radio ... Mira ... No! No! Not that switch!

Message Three
Hello ... hello ... Professor Storm here. Mira is naughtier now! She sometimes eats my dinner. She often opens cupboards ... Mira! ...

Message Four
Help! ... Please ... Storm here! Mira is impossible! She always jumps on my bed in the morning. She often swings from the lamp, and she always teases my cat, and ... often breaks things ... Miiirrraa!

Lesson 4

OBJECTIVES:to discover information; to ask about habits; consolidation of *do* as auxiliary verb
TARGET LANGUAGE: *Do you ... ?*
RECYCLED LANGUAGE: *always, often, sometimes, never*
MATERIALS: cassette recorder, cassette 2, photocopies of resource page 148

13 PERSONALITY QUIZ: Read and answer. Look and write. —

1 This is a humorous activity. It is advisable not to refer back to the previous activities on Mira the monkey in order to sustain the humour in this activity.
2 Read through the questions with the class and check comprehension.
3 Let the children answer individually by colouring in the appropriate number of circles to 'find out their personality'.
4 When they have finished, focus attention on the score key below the questions and let them work out their individual scores.
5 In pairs they can work out their partner's score by asking him/her the questions and colouring the circles; the other child will answer simply *always, sometimes,* etc.
6 Depending on their scores they can solve the puzzle revealing their personality!

Key
The symbols all correspond to letters which are shown somewhere in the hidden sentence, e.g. a blue star corresponds to the letter A.
30–40 points: Are you sure you're not a little monkey?
20–29 points: Sometimes you are very good, but sometimes ... !
1–19 points: You're always an angel.

Extension: personality questionnaire

This pairs activity will provide additional practice of the adverbs of frequency and *Do you ... ?* questions.

1 Hand out copies of resource page 148 and read through the questions briefly with the class.
2 Let the children fill in the first grid about themselves – as honestly and truthfully as they wish!
3 Have the children swap grids with a friend who then completes the second form from his/her partner's grid.
4 If there is time, some of them could be read out to the rest of the class, omitting the name, so that the others have to guess who is being described.
5 A further development is for pairs of children to prepare other sets of questions of the same sort, and then ask and answer them in the same way.

Drama time

9 The Prince of Arion (See page 10 of the Introduction for notes on *Drama time* for the story.)

RESCUE!

Story time

See page 9 of the Introduction for more suggestions on dealing with the story.

1   Remind the children of the story so far and invite suggestions as to what they think is going to happen.

2   Focus attention on the title *Rescue!*, and in L1 ask if anyone knows what this means. Explain the title and ask why they think the episode is called *Rescue!*, accepting all suggestions for the moment.

3   Remind the children of where Ben and his friends are trying to go and why (*back to the spaceship with the materials necessary to repair the spaceship*) and how they think they might regain control of the capsule. Accept all answers for the moment.

4   Using the scenes, introduce the word *funfair.* Ask if they have been to a funfair. Ask questions like *Do you like funfairs? What's your favourite ride?* Write the names of some of the rides on the board and ask *Are you afraid of the (Roller Coaster, Big Wheel, Ghost Train, etc.)?*

5   Get them to look at the pictures in this episode. Ask the children what they think is taking place. Encourage them to describe what they see in the scenes in English. Where possible focus on those items that the children have recently learnt. Make sure that they have understood that:

   a   Jasper has inadvertently switched off the automatic pilot and Kanda is having difficulty controlling the capsule.

   b   the capsule has entered a funfair and is passing under the roller coaster, through the tunnel, over the bridge.

   c   Kanda realises that the automatic pilot has been switched off.

   d   Ben tells Jasper not to touch the automatic pilot button.

   e   the capsule heads into space and comes to a halt near the spaceship.

   f   the capsule is recovered by the mother ship.

   g   the children have all arrived safe and sound and are reunited with the adults.

   h   Ben, Toby and Susan are proud of having found all the materials needed.

   i   while Kanda shows Ben, Susan and Jasper around the spaceship, Rui, Marla and Doctor Alpha repair the computer.

   j   the repairs are successful and energy is restored.

   k   Marla, Rui and Kanda say thank you and goodbye to them, and Doctor Alpha, Jasper and the children are beamed back to Earth.

   l   Rui, Marla and Kanda set course for their return to Arion.

6   Follow the *Story time* procedure on page 9 of the Introduction. Play the tape and ask the children to follow the story on the book.

7   Play the tape again. This time they have to listen out for:

   a   where the control for the automatic pilot is (*It's on the right!*).

   b   why Kanda is afraid when they get near the spaceship (*It's all dark!*).

   c   how Doctor Alpha asks Ben if they managed to get the materials (*Have you got the materials?*).

   d   how Kanda invites Ben and the others to see the spaceship (*Do you want to see the spaceship?*).

   To help the children find the answers to these comprehension questions, stop the tape just before the relevant section of the dialogue.

Lesson 1

OBJECTIVES: to describe and give instructions for movement
TARGET LANGUAGE: prepositions of movement (*under, over, through, up, down, around, across*)
RECYCLED LANGUAGE: features of the countryside (*lake, bridge, tunnel, mountain*)
MATERIALS: cassette recorder, cassette 2, photocopies of resource pages 149–150

Introduction

Encourage the children to describe the movement of the capsule when it got into the funfair, and as they do so illustrate their description with mime gestures. These gestures will serve later on as cues for the children to produce the new language items, e.g. for *under* move one hand under the other describing an arc.

1 Listen and repeat. Listen and mime.

See page 13 of the Introduction for more information on the *Listen and repeat* activities.

1 The children observe the flashback scene and listen and repeat.
2 Model and drill the dialogue.
3 Focus the attention on the drawings below the flashback scene. Tell the children they are going to learn how to say these movements.
4 The children listen to the tape. The first time they follow with their fingers.

Tapescript

under over through up down around across

5 The second time, stop the tape after each word and show the children the gesture that illustrates the meaning. Get the children to repeat it several times.

> **FINGER MIMING: all the movements can be mimed by walking the fingers of your right hand in the various directions on the open palm of your left hand to illustrate the movements. *Across* will require you to change the position of your hand to contrast with *through*.**

6 In pairs, child A closes his/her eyes and holds up his/her hand with open palm. Child B 'walks' his/her fingers following the movements of the mime. Child A has to call out the movement he/she feels. E.g. child B walks his fingers up A's hand. Child A has to call out *Up!*

Escape door: the funfair

1 Hand out copies of resource page 149. This resource material is useful for revising, in a new attractive context, much of the language the children are familiar with.
2 Focus attention on the funfair and identify the various rides. Model and drill the *Big Wheel, the Water Splash, the Ghost Train* and the *Roller Coaster.* Ask e.g. *Look at the Water Splash: where does the boat go?* Elicit *It goes down the hill, across the lake, through the tunnel,* etc. Do the same for the other rides. Then the children can write a description of the

RESCUE!

route taken by the *Water Splash*. (The other rides only produce limited movement.)

3 Allow the children a few moments to observe the funfair scene. Tell them they are going to listen to questions about the picture and they will have to answer them when they hear a sound and a pause (*) If they need more time, pause or stop the tape after each question to give them chance to find and call out the answers.

Tapescript

Welcome to the funfair. Look at the picture.
How many children are there? (*) (eighteen)
This boy has got black hair. He's buying a ticket. What number is he? (*) (1)
Look at the two boys on the right... number 5 and number 6. Which one is stronger? (*) (6)
Look at boy number 2. What's he doing? (*) (He's buying an ice cream.)
Look at the ice cream. How much is it? (*) (99p)
There's a clown in the picture. What number is he? (*) (4)
How many boys are listening to the clown? (*) (two; The third is a girl.)
Number 3 is the Ghost Train. How much is the ticket for the Ghost Train? (*) (£1.50)
In the Ghost Train tunnel, what can you see? (*) (Monsters, witches, ghosts, bats, spiders)
Look at number 7. This is the Water Splash. Who's going on the Water Splash, a boy or a girl? (*) (a girl) Is she afraid? (*) (No)
Look at number 8. This is the Roller Coaster. How many cars are on the Roller Coaster? (*) (Two)
Look at the Roller Coaster again. Where's the second car? (*) (On the bridge)
Look at number 9. This is the Big Wheel. Is the boy on the left or the right? (*) (right)
If you want to go on the Big Wheel, how much is the ticket? (*) (£1.00)
How much is the ticket for the Roller Coaster? (*) (£2.50)
You've got two pounds. Where can you go? (*) (On the Water Splash, Ghost Train, Big Wheel)
Look at girl number 10. Do you think she wants to go on the Ghost Train or on the Water Splash? (*) (The Ghost Train)
Look at number 11. Where does he want to go? (*) (On the Water Splash)

4 Hand out photocopies of resource page 150. The children cut out the speech bubbles, then they decide who's saying what and stick the speech bubbles in the appropriate position.

Key

I'm stronger than you! (6)	I'd like an ice cream, please. (2)
One ticket, please. (1)	I want to go on the Ghost Train. (10)
Let's go on the Water Splash! (11)	
Whoopeeee! Hi, everyone! Welcome to Funland! Ha ha ha! My name's Bonzo ... (4)	

2 Read and match.

1 The children look at the picture and describe the objects shown in detail. Ask *What's this?* The children answer *It's a/the hill/tunnel/mountain/hill/bridge/Earth/lake*.
2 Focus attention on the Roller Coaster car and ask *Where does the car go?* Elicit *It goes up (the hill)*, etc. The children match the picture with the corresponding description.

Key

up (the hill)	through the tunnel	around the mountain	down (the mountain)
around the Earth	across the lake	over the bridge	

3 Look and describe.

Ask the children to describe the Roller Coaster ride. They can start with *It goes... .*

4 SONG: Fly!

See page 15 of the Introduction for more suggestions on dealing with songs and raps.

Hand out copies of resource page 151. Let them read the words of the song, and match the pictures to the relevant descriptions.

Lesson 2

OBJECTIVES:	to talk about rules and regulations
TARGET LANGUAGE:	*must/mustn't*
RECYCLED LANGUAGE:	imperatives
MATERIALS:	cassette recorder, cassette 2

Introduction

1 Ask the children if they remember some of the things you and other teachers tell them to do/not to do during their lessons or while they are at school. Elicit *Don't talk! Be quiet! Don't copy! Don't run! Write neatly!* etc.

2 Explain that every place has rules and that they are going to learn how we explain that there is a rule or the necessity to do something.

5 Listen and repeat.

See page 13 of the Introduction for more information on the *Listen and repeat* activities.

1 Focus attention on the first flashback where Kanda asks Ben and his friends to wear the seat belts as the capsule is going very fast.

2 Ask the children to listen first, and then repeat the model sentences.

3 In the second flashback, remind the children of when the space capsule went out of control and what instruction Ben gave Jasper to avoid the same thing happening again.

4 Again, the children listen and then repeat the model sentences.

6 Listen and point. Listen and match.

1 Focus attention on the first picture and ask *Who do you think she is? How many children are there? What are they doing?* etc. to elicit that a teacher is accompanying a group of children to the swimming pool.

2 Explain that the teacher is asking the children if they know what the pictures mean.

3 Tell them they are going to listen to the tape and they have to find out what they mean.

Tapescript

Teacher   OK, children. Here we are. We're at the swimming pool. There are some rules to follow. Now look at this poster. Look at the first picture: you can see two feet and a shower ... what's the rule?

Patrick   You must wash your feet!

Teacher	That's right! Good! And what can you see in the second picture, Debbie?
Debbie	I think it's a head.
Teacher	Yes. Anything else?
Debbie	Yes ... a special cap ... Yes! I know! You must wear a cap!
Teacher	Very good! So what are the rules, Mark?
Mark	You must wash your feet and you must wear a cap.
Teacher	Excellent! Now look here, on the right. There's a big cross on two legs. What does it mean, Milly?
Milly	That's easy! You mustn't run!
Teacher	That's right! And the other?
Grant	There's a pair of shoes and a cross ... it means you mustn't wear shoes!
Teacher	Great! So ... you mustn't run and you mustn't wear your shoes. OK? ... Let's go in! ...

4 For the second part of the activity, focus attention on the five scenes and encourage the children to identify them (a school, a train, a street, a picnic area, a safari park).

5 Tell the children that there are some rules which relate to these areas. There are two for each picture, one with *must* and one with *mustn't*.

6 Let the children listen to the rules without indicating which scenes they refer to.

7 Now the children listen and read them again individually and write the number corresponding to the most appropriate place next to the rule. They then check in pairs.

8 Look at the scenes again and ask the class if there are any other rules they can think of for these situations.

Tapescript

1 You mustn't put your head out of the window.
3 You mustn't run.
5 You must listen to the teacher.
7 You must stay in the car.
9 You must look left and right.
Can you think of more rules?

2 You must take your litter home.
4 You mustn't open the car window.
6 You mustn't climb trees.
8 You mustn't play in the road.
10 You must have a ticket.

Lesson 3

OBJECTIVES:	to talk about rules and regulations; to explain a route to follow
TARGET LANGUAGE:	*must/mustn't, wall, rock*
RECYCLED LANGUAGE:	*up, down, round, across, over, through, around* features of the countryside (*tree, bridge, bushes, lake, rocks, gate, cave, rope*)
MATERIALS:	cassette recorder, cassette 2, paper fastener or drawing pins, photocopies of resource page 152

7 Listen and repeat. Listen and choose.

See page 13 of the Introduction for more information on the *Listen and repeat* activities.

1 Focus attention on the Adventure Circuit. Explain that in the funfair there is an exciting attraction that children love, and it is called the Adventure Circuit. Every day there is a competition where the winner gets free tickets for the funfair. The illustration shows some children trying out the circuit.

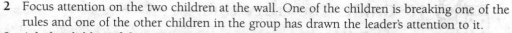

2 Focus attention on the two children at the wall. One of the children is breaking one of the rules and one of the other children in the group has drawn the leader's attention to it.

3 Ask the children if they can suggest which rule has not been followed. *(You must go over the wall.)*

4 Play the first part of the message twice. The first time they find out which child is Andy (the one going round the wall). The second time focus attention on how the leader tells Andy what to do. *(You must ... .)*

5 Let the children listen and repeat the model sentence.

6 Tell them they are going to listen Mr. Green explaining the whole route. They must tick the box that corresponds to the right action. Stop the tape if necessary where it is marked (/).

Tapescript

Mr. Green Right! Quiet please. Now listen carefully ... this is what you must do.
You mustn't go round the wall, you must go over the wall. (/) Then you must run around the tree three times. (/) OK. At the bridge ... you must go over the bridge. (/) and then you must go up and down the hill ... you mustn't go around it ... Andy! (/) Then, things get difficult! There's a second bridge ... you mustn't go over it! You must go down the slide and climb up the rope.

Children Oh no! Aah!

Mr. Green Remember you must go down the slide and up the rope! (/) Then you must go through the bushes. (/) You mustn't stop ... and after that you must go across the lake – walking on the rocks! (/) Then you come to a gate ... and you must go under the gate ... (/) Then at the rock, you must jump over the rock ... (/) and you're on the last section. There's a cave.

Children Oooh! Aah! Wow!

Mr. Green You must go through the cave. (/) Then you must touch the buzzer to stop the clock. OK?

Children Yeah! Great! Let's go!

7 Check with the class. Get the children to go over the circuit telling you what you must do. They then draw in the right route.

8 Look and describe.

1 The children work in pairs. They must describe the alternative route taking it in turns to say the sentences, e.g.
   A *You must go round the wall.*
   B *You must go/climb up the tree.*

2 Ask the children to compare the two routes and ask them *Do you think it's easy or difficult?* Let them explain their reasons in L1.

9 PROJECT: Classroom rules

1 Elicit classroom rules involving *must* and *mustn't*. Here are some suggestions:
   We mustn't eat chewing gum in class/chatter/run in the corridor/use bad language/fight/copy/be late/shout/write on the desks, etc.
   We must do our homework/ask the teacher before we leave the room/put up our hands before speaking/pay attention/put things away/behave well/wear trainers in the gym, etc.

2 Help the children with any new language they need.

3 When they have decided on the rules they want to include, make an illustrated wall chart.

RESCUE!

10 GAME: The crazy club!

See page 15 of the Introduction for more suggestions on dealing with games.

1 The children work in small groups. The aim of the game is to make a list of imaginary rules for their group (or club).
2 Ask the children to draw a wheel like the one on their book. Draw attention to the colours and to the fact that the completion of each sentence is in a sector of the same colour as the verb. They can invent their own sentences, but have to stick to the colour codes.
3 When the wheel is ready, they put the paper fastener or drawing pin through the spot marked, inserting from the back so that the pointer spins easily on the point. For the size of the pointer, they can copy the model in their books.
4 Explain the rules of the game, which are as follows:
   a for each new rule the children have to invent, they spin the pointer three times:
      1 the first spin indicates if the rule is with *must* or *mustn't*.
      2 the second spin indicates the verb.
      3 the third spin indicates how to finish the sentence; the completion of the sentence is in the sector of the same colour as the verb.
   b each group writes the rules as they come up. The minimum number is four, but the children can make more by repeating a verb.
   c make sure that one rule doesn't contradict another! E.g. *must/mustn't have a pet*.
   d when they have finished they stick their club rules on the board and together they decide which club is the craziest!

Extension: join our club!

Indicate one of the clubs on the board and ask one child *Do you want to join this club?* Encourage him/her to answer with, e.g. *No, I don't, because (I don't like snails!)*. *No, I can't, because I (haven't got an English coin)*. *Yes, I do! I like (chips)*, etc.
The children could find out which club attracts the greatest membership!

11 SONG: Nothing

See page 15 of the Introduction for more suggestions on dealing with songs and raps.

1 Hand out copies of resource page 152. Let the children read the words of the song and look at the pictures.
2 Play the song. The children listen and point to the pictures illustrating the activities mentioned. Check that they have understood the actions described. Play the song again, this time the children listen and mime the actions.
3 Proceed in the usual way, by letting the children join once they are confident with the words.

Lesson 4

> OBJECTIVES: to talk about the past; to say where you were and ask where other people were
> TARGET LANGUAGE: *I was ..., Where were you ... ?*
> RECYCLED LANGUAGE: places, (*room, airport, Earth, toy shop, cave*)
> MATERIALS: cassette recorder, cassette 2, photocopies of resource page 153

12 Listen and repeat. Look and match.

See page 13 of the Introduction for more information on the *Listen and repeat* activities.

1 Tell the class they are going to listen to the characters talking about various moments in the story. Ask them to listen first, and then repeat the model sentences.

2 Point to one of the scenes and the children try to remember what the character said, e.g. *Toby said 'I was at the airport!'*

3 Tell the children that the numbers in the centre refer to the various episodes (units) in the story. They have to try and match each scene with the right episode number. This can be done as a race, without consulting their books as they do it. Alternatively the children can go back and check the storyline to find the scenes.

Tapescript and key

Susan	I was near a toyshop.	Unit 5
Ben	I was in a cave.	Unit 9
Toby	I was at the airport.	Unit 2
Ben	I was in a tunnel.	Unit 7
Doctor Alpha	I was in the sitting room.	Unit 2
Kanda	I was near Earth.	Unit 1
Doctor Alpha	I was in the spaceship.	Unit 3
Ben	I was at the station.	Unit 6

13 Read and write the letter.

1 Focus attention on the six sentences and let the children read through them.

2 Explain that these sentences describe where the people were and correspond to the drawings above.

3 The children read each sentence and write the letter corresponding to the drawing in the box provided.

14 Listen and choose.

1 The children look at the scenes in their books. Elicit the names of the places shown.

2 Tell them they are going to listen to some children saying where they were yesterday, but their voices have been masked by a secret scrambler. Give an example by 'speaking' with your mouth closed, pointing to a child's book and with suitable mime ask *Can I have your book, please?* Ask the class what they thought you said.

3 The children have to guess and say the sentence that the speaker is saying. They will be helped by the intonation and the number of syllables in the phrases and the subsequent sound effect.

RESCUE!

4   Let them listen to the sentences one at a time, and stop the tape after the sound effect.

Tapescript and key
I was at the swimming pool. I was at the airport. I was at the cinema.
I was at the museum. I was at school.

15 GAME: Find your group

See page 15 of the Introduction for more suggestions on dealing with games.

1   For this activity you will need pictures of five places; you can use some of the place cards from resource page 153. Make sure that each child has a photocopied picture of one of the places.

2   The children go round the class and say, e.g. *I was at the cinema,* according to the picture on their cards. If the other child says an identical phrase, they link arms and move around together looking for children who were also in the same place.

3   At the end of the activity there should be five groups of children each of whom were in the same place.

16 Listen and repeat.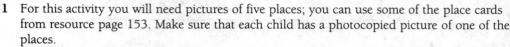

See page 13 of the Introduction for more information on the *Listen and repeat* activities.

1   Ask the children to look at the presentation flash. Explain that a detective is questioning three suspects and wants to know their movements yesterday at 4 o'clock. Encourage the children to suggest what questions he might ask.

2   Play the tape, while the children listen and point. Ask them why the last person said *Ooops!* (He has given the game away!)

3   Play the tape and focus attention on the question.

4   Play the tape again. Model the dialogue using chain drilling.

5   Tell them that now the detective (you) is going to interrogate some more suspects (the children!). Tell them to look back at the previous page and choose a place they 'were' yesterday.

   T *Where were you yesterday afternoon?*
   A *I was in the spaceship!*
   T *Where were you yesterday afternoon?*
   B *I was at the swimming pool.* etc.

6   Now let them continue this around the class, answering the question, then asking it of the next child.

   B *I was at the swimming pool. Where were you yesterday afternoon?*
   C *I was at the cinema. Where were you yesterday afternoon?*
   D *I was at the toy shop. Where ... ,* etc.

17 Listen and link.

1   Focus attention on the tickets, and ask the children to tell you what information they can find in each one. Ask questions like *What's this? Is this ticket for the museum or for the cinema? How much is the ticket for the swimming pool? What colour is the ticket for the amusement arcade?* Focus attention on the cinema ticket and ask *Is this a ticket for a child or for an adult?* Ask *What time does the amusement arcade open?*

2   Tell the children that the detective is questioning four suspects about their movements yesterday afternoon (Sunday). One of them is not telling the truth. They will have to listen and check the information each suspect gives.

3 Play the tape. The first time they listen they link each character with the tickets according to where they say they were. The second time they try to identify the person who is not telling the truth.

4 The solution is contained in the last section of the tape so don't play this section until you are ready to give the children the answer.

Tapescript

Detective	Right. I want to ask you about yesterday afternoon ... Sunday. What's your name, please?
Bob Wilson	Bob. Bob Wilson.
Detective	Right, Mr Wilson, where were you yesterday afternoon?
Bob	Yesterday afternoon? Sunday? Oh yes, I was at the cinema ... it was a great film! Oh, here's my ticket!
Detective	OK. ... yes ... thank you ...
Detective	Now ... you are ... Sharon Silver?
Sharon	Yes. What's the matter?
Detective	I'd like to ask you some questions, please.
Sharon	OK.
Detective	Now, where were you yesterday afternoon?
Sharon	Let me think ... oh ... yes ... I was at the museum ... it was very interesting.
Detective	Have you got a ticket?
Sharon	Oh ... yes, here it is!
Detective	Thank you.
Detective	What's your name, please?
Alan	Alan, Alan Martin.
Detective	Where were you yesterday afternoon, Mr Martin?
Alan	I was at the swimming pool ... with my sister ...
Detective	At the swimming pool? Can I see your ticket?
Alan	Just a moment ... Where is it? ... Here!
Detective	Right, thank you.
Hal	Hello, I'm Hal Thomson.
Detective	Thank you, Mr. Thomson. Where were you yesterday afternoon?
Hal	Sunday? Er ... oh yes, I was at the new amusement arcade in London Road ... I like electronic games and computers ... I always go there on Sunday!
Detective	I see ... right ... have you got a ticket or something?
Hal	Ticket? I haven't got a ticket but I've got this ...
Detective	Thank you ... Mmmm ... OK.
Detective	Sharon Silver ... you're under arrest! Officer!
Officer	Yes, sir?
Detective	Take her to the police station!
Sharon	No! Let me go!

Key

Sharon Silver is under arrest because she said she was at the museum and the ticket states that the museum is closed on Sunday.

RESCUE!

18 GAME: Where were you at ...?

See page 15 of the Introduction for more suggestions on dealing with games.

1 Hand out photocopies of resource pages 153–154. There are eleven place cards, twelve question/ time cards and one joker, which can be used as either a place or question/time card, as necessary. Ask the children to cut out the pictures, back them with card and colour them.

2 Explain the rules of the game, which are as follows:

a the children play in pairs. One of them shuffles the cards and deals them out, twelve each.

b the child who did not deal the cards starts the game. Providing he/she has a question card, he/she may start the game by putting it down on the desk and asking *Where were you at ... ?* (the time shown on the card).

c the other child chooses one of his/her place cards, puts it down and answers appropriately *I was at the ...* (place shown on the card).

d he/she then continues the game by asking a new question to which the other player must respond.

e if a player has no question/time cards or no answer cards, and no joker either, he/she must say *Pass* and the other player has the chance to put down one of his/her cards and then ask another question.

f the winner is the child who manages to put down all his/her cards first.

19 Look and write.

1 This activity can be done in pairs. The cards used for the game in Activity 18 above should be divided into two groups; question/time cards and place cards, each placed face down.

2 The children turn over a question/time card, say and write the corresponding question, e.g. *Where were you at five o'clock?*

3 They then turn over a place card, say and write the corresponding answer, e.g. *I was at the cinema.*

Drama time

10 Rescue! (See page 10 of the Introduction for notes on *Drama time* for the story.)

11 HOME AGAIN!

Story time

See page 13 of the Introduction for more suggestions on dealing with the story.

1 Remind the children of the story so far. Ask them about the last scene, e.g. *Where was Rui?*
(*He was in the spaceship.*) Ask the children *Where do you think Ben and Jasper are now?*

2 Tell them that this is the last episode in the story, and invite suggestions as to what they
think is going to happen. Focus attention on the title *Home Again!,* and ask what they
think *home* refers to: Ben's home or Kanda's or both.

3 Using the illustrations, introduce useful items for enabling the children to talk about the
scenes, e.g. *throne, pretend/lie, minister, prison.* Model and drill them.

4 Get them to look at the pictures and ask them what they think is taking place. Encourage
them to describe what they see in the scenes in English. Where possible focus on those
items that the children have recently learnt. Make sure that they have understood that:

   a Damek Za is back on Arion and intends to become king.
   b he is telling the ministers that Rui, Marla and Kanda were all killed in a terrible
   accident.
   c the ministers know Damek Za is evil and are reluctant to crown him.
   d Rui, Marla and Kanda arrive and expose Damek Za, who is taken off to prison.
   e they tell the ministers about their encounter with the people from Earth.
   f Kanda describes the Earth people and Jasper.
   g Marla, Rui and Kanda will never forget Doctor Alpha, Ben and his friends.
   h Doctor Alpha, the children and Jasper have all arrived home safely and are excitedly
   talking about their adventure.
   i Uncle Otto arrives home, and is delighted to see everyone.
   j he has found a sphere in the garden which he believes is one of the children's toys.
   k this sphere has come from Arion and while Doctor Alpha is talking to Otto, the
   children open it.
   l the sphere contains a thank-you present from Arion: special coins showing their faces.

5 Follow the *Story time* procedure on page 9 of the Introduction. Play the tape and ask the
children to follow the story on the book.

6 Play the tape again. This time they have to listen out for:

   a why Damek Za thinks he should be king (*I'm Rui's brother!*).
   b what instruction he gives the minister (*Bring me the crown!*).
   c what the minister says when Damek Za demands the crown (*What shall we do?*).
   d what information Marla gives the ministers about Doctor Alpha, the children and
   Jasper (*They live on a planet called Earth*).
   e what information Kanda gives about people from Earth (*They're bigger than us*).
   f what questions Ben asks himself as he looks up into the sky (*Where are they now? Are
   they all right?*).
   g why Otto is sorry (*I wasn't at the airport*).

HOME AGAIN!

Lesson 1

OBJECTIVES:	to ask and talk about people's intentions
TARGET LANGUAGE:	*I'm going to (be)..., What are you going to be?* jobs *(painter, ballerina, astronaut, footballer, actor/actress, teacher, vet), famous*
RECYCLED LANGUAGE:	*queen, detective*
MATERIALS:	cassette recorder, cassette 2

Introduction

Remind the children of what happened in the story and ask them what Damek Za has just decided in this particular scene (*to be king*). Ask if he is king at the moment (*No*). This is to clarify the concept of future intention.

1 Listen and repeat. Listen and match.

See page 13 of the Introduction for more information on the *Listen and repeat* activities.

1 Focus attention on the flashback illustrating Damek Za's intention (taken from page 82 of the last episode). Tell them they are going to listen to how Damek Za expresses this intention. The children listen to and repeat the first part of the tape.
2 Focus attention on the drawings. Give the children time to study the pictures and ask if they recognise any of them. Tell them that these children are giving us some clues as to what they would like to be when they grow up.
3 Tell them they are going to listen to the children talking about this. The children listen and point to each child in turn.
4 They then listen and repeat. Model and drill each sentence.

Tapescript

1 I'm going to be a detective.   2 I'm going to be Queen.
3 I'm going to be a painter.   4 I'm going to be a ballerina.
5 I'm going to be a super-hero.   6 I'm going to be an astronaut.

5 Say the sentences in random order and the children have to call out the corresponding number of the picture.
6 Mime one of the jobs and let them call out what that child says, e.g. *I'm going to be Queen.*
7 In pairs, one child points to one of the drawings and the other says what that child is saying.
8 Focus attention on the photos and tell the children that these are the same children but now grown up. Explain that they have all achieved their childhood ambitions. Read the names with the class and ask if they know anything about these characters.
9 Tell the children they are going to listen again. This time they have to identify the speaker and match the picture to the corresponding photo.

Key

detective – Sherlock Holmes   queen – Cleopatra
painter – Pablo Picasso   ballerina – Carla Fracci
super-hero – Hercules   astronaut – Valentina Tereshkova

2 Listen and tick.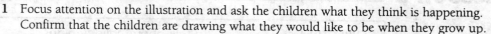

1 Focus attention on the illustration and ask the children what they think is happening. Confirm that the children are drawing what they would like to be when they grow up.

2 Ask the class what they think the teacher is asking and what the child is saying. Explain that the teacher is asking the child what he wants to be when he grows up. The child is answering that he intends to become a professional footballer.

3 Focus attention on the grid and read the names of the characters and the jobs. Model and drill *actor/actress* and *vet* as these are new items.

4 Explain that the teacher is going to ask these six children the same question. The children listen to the interview and put a tick in the appropriate box.

Tapescript

Teacher	Very nice. What have we got here? They're really good ... is this your drawing, Kevin?
Kevin	Yes, I'm going to be a detective ... just like Sherlock Holmes!
Teacher	Right! Have you finished, Nick?
Nick	No, not yet ...
Teacher	What are you going to be?
Nick	I like the theatre and the cinema ... I'm going to be an actor! I'm going to be famous!
Teacher	Good luck! Now ... what about you, Alan? What are you going to be?
Alan	I'm very good at football ... I'm going to be a footballer. Manchester United is my favourite team ... yes ... I'm going to play for Manchester!
Jill	Manchester United?! Rubbish!!
Teacher	Now Jill. What are you going to be? A teacher?
Jill	No! Not a teacher! I'm going to be a pilot. I'm going to travel around the world ... America, Europe, Africa ...
Teacher	Mmmm, to be a pilot, you must be good at geography! What about you, Anna?
Anna	I love animals! At home I've got five pets: a dog, two cats, a rabbit and a tortoise! I'm going to be a vet ...
Teacher	That's interesting. OK. And you, Barbara? What are you going to be?
Barbara	You!
Teacher	What?! Me?!
Barbara	Yes! I'm going to be a teacher!
Teacher	Fine! Now, for homework ...

3 Ask and answer.

1 Remind the children of the question the teacher asked in the previous activity (*What are you going to be?*). Ask the children to repeat this model question.

2 In pairs, they imagine they are one of the children of the previous activity and follow this model dialogue:

   A *What are you going to be?*
   B *I'm going to be a (vet).*
   A *You're (Anna)!*
   B *Yes, that's right!/No!*

3 When they have finished, ask the children about their own intentions/ambitions about their future. Ask *What are you going to be, (Luca)?* Provide any necessary vocabulary for the children to answer.

HOME AGAIN!

Lesson 2

OBJECTIVES:	to talk about holiday plans
TARGET LANGUAGE:	*Where/How/What are you going to ...?*, holidays (*at the seaside, in the country, abroad, go sightseeing, go cycling/walking*)
RECYCLED LANGUAGE:	the countryside, means of transport
MATERIALS:	cassette recorder, cassette 2, photocopies of resource material pages 155–157

Introduction

1 Ask the children *When do the summer holidays start?* Show them on the calendar when this period is to reinforce the idea that they are talking about the future. Say *Look! Now it's (the month) and the holidays are in ... months/weeks.*

2 Explain that during the summer holidays many people go away to various destinations, and, of course, this involves planning. Ask the children what aspects of holidays are decided in advance, e.g. where to go, how to travel, what to do there and, therefore, what to take.

4 Listen and point. Listen and repeat.

See page 13 of the Introduction for more information on the *Listen and repeat* activities.

1 Ask the children to observe the four sets of drawings on page 87. Ask them to predict what kind of questions they will hear.

2 Play the tape and ask the children to listen and point.

3 The second time they listen and repeat.

Tapescript

One

Adult 1	Where are you going to spend your holidays?
Child 1	At the seaside.
Adult 2	Where are you going to spend your holidays?
Child 2	In the country.
Adult 3	Where are you going to spend your holidays?
Child 3	At home.
Adult 4	Where are you going to spend your holidays?
Child 4	Abroad.
Adult 5	Where are you going to spend your holidays?
Child 5	In the mountains.
Adult 6	Where are you going to spend your holidays?
Child 6	At the lake.

Two

Adult 1	How are you going to get there?
Child 1	By ship.
Adult 2	How are you going to get there?
Child 2	By coach.
Adult 4	How are you going to get there?

Child 4	By plane.
Adult 5	How are you going to get there?
Child 5	By train.
Adult 6	How are you going to get there?
Child 6	By car.

Three

Adult 1	What are you going to take?
Child 1	My surfboard.
Adult 2	What are you going to take?
Child 2	My sunglasses.
Adult 4	What are you going to take?
Child 4	My camera.
Adult 5	What are you going to take?
Child 5	My tracksuit.
Adult 6	What are you going to take?
Child 6	My cap.

Four

Adult 4	What are you going to do?
Child 4	Go sightseeing.
Adult 1	What are you going to do?
Child 1	Go swimming.
Adult 5	What are you going to do?
Child 5	Go walking.
Adult 3	What are you going to do?
Child 3	Play with my friends.
Adult 2	What are you going to do?
Child 2	Go cycling.

5 Ask and answer.

1 In pairs, child A starts with question 1 *Where are you going to spend your holidays?* Child B points to one of the drawings in that section and gives a suitable reply, e.g. *At the seaside.*
2 Child A then asks all four questions, then the two children swap over.

6 SONG: Holiday rap

See page 15 of the Introduction for more information on dealing with song and raps.

1 This rap is aimed at providing the children both with fluency practice and a complete model for expressing intentions.
2 Hand out photocopies of resource page 155. Tell the children that they are going to listen and they have to identify which pictures best illustrate Susan's plans.
3 Start the rap without the tape and let the children gradually build up the speed as they get more and more familiar with the words and the rhythm.

7 Listen and place.

1 Hand out photocopies of resource page 156 and give each child a copy. Tell the children to colour and then cut out the items surrounded by a dotted line.
2 Focus attention on the three scenes and ask the children if they recognise the locations (*seaside, mountain* and *city: Paris*). Focus attention on the cutouts and make sure the

111

HOME AGAIN!

children are familiar with the vocabulary: *guitar, diary, comics, camera, surfboard, video camera/handcam, sunglasses, bike.*

3 Explain that a child is doing a survey on plans for the holidays. Elicit what questions she might ask, like *Where are you going to spend your holidays? How are you going to get there? What are you going to take? What are you going to do?*

4 The children listen to the tape and place the cutouts in the appropriate place in each scene according to what they hear on the tape.

Tapescript

Child	Oh, Natalie! Natalie!
Natalie	Yes? Just a minute ... OK.
Child	Can you help me? I'm doing a survey and I'd like to ask you some questions.
Natalie	Oh, all right. What questions?
Child	Well, where are you going to spend your holidays?
Natalie	This year? In the mountains. I'm going to go in August.
Child	... In the mountains ... OK ... and ... how are you going to get there?
Natalie	By car, because there isn't a station.
Child	What are you going to take?
Natalie	Well, warm clothes of course and ... oh yes, I'm going to take my guitar ... I like playing the guitar in the evening with my friends ...
Child	And ... ?
Natalie	I'm going to take my camera this year, because there are some beautiful animals to photograph ... I love animals ... and I'm going to take some books and comics ...
Child	What are you going to do in the mountains?
Natalie	Well, there are lots of things to do ... I'm going to go walking with my Mum, and I'm going to play with my friends ... I've got lots of friends in the mountains ...
Child	Thanks, Natalie. Bye! ... Oh, Liz! Just in time! Liz, can I ask you some questions?
Liz	Sure ... what are you doing?
Child	I'm doing a survey about holidays.
Liz	Holidays? I'm going to go to Paris!
Child	Wow! How are you going to get there?
Liz	By plane ... it's the first time for me ...
Child	Paris ... by plane ... OK ... what are you going to take?
Liz	I'm going to take my Dad's video camera ... and ... oh yes, I'm going to take my French dictionary.
Child	Do you speak French, Liz?
Liz	Mmm, only a little, we're studying it at school this year ... and, what else ...? Oh yes, I'm going to take my diary ... I always take my diary.
Child	What are you going to do in Paris?
Liz	I'm going to go sightseeing ... I want to see the Eiffel Tower ...
Child	Right. Great! Thanks Liz. See you.
Child	Now, who shall I ask? Oh yes! There's Tina. Hi, Tina!
Tina	Hello?
Child	Tina, where are you going to spend your holidays?
Tina	At the seaside. I always go to the seaside in summer.
Child	How are you going to get there?
Tina	By train ... it's a long way.
Child	What are you going to take?
Tina	Oh ... the usual things ... I'm going to take my sunglasses, my camera ... and ... oh yes, my new surfboard ... and my bike ...

Child	OK ... sunglasses – camera – bike ... right!
Tina	... and my surfboard!
Child	Oh yes, thanks. What are you going to do there?
Tina	I'm going to go swimming – every day! I love swimming ... and I'm going to go cycling in the evening ...
Child	Great! That's all! Thanks, Tina. Bye!
Tina	Bye!

8 SURVEY: Holidays

1 Using the questions from the previous activities, the children carry out a survey along the guidelines of the previous activity.

2 Tell the children to plan their ideal holiday. Give them a few minutes to 'plan', and make a note of what they have decided.

3 Put the following grid on the board and have the children copy it so that they can record the information they gather.

	(Name)	(Name)	(Name)
Where are you going to spend your holidays?			
How are you going to get there?			
What are you going to take?			
What are you going to do?			

Extension: holiday plans

The children write a description of their plans for the coming holiday period using the following model: *This year I'm going to spend my holidays ... . I'm going to get there by ... . I'm going to take ... . I'm going to ... .*

GAME: Fortune teller

1 Ask the children if they have ever seen a fortune teller at a fair. Discuss what sort of things he/she tells you. Tell them they are going to play a game in which they will be the fortune teller and discover some interesting things about what the future holds for them!!!

2 Hand out copies of resource page 157. Read the cards with the children. Focus attention on the drawings in the crystal balls asking *What can you see?* Read the sentence below, check comprehension and then let them repeat the sentence.

3 The children play in pairs. The cards are shuffled and placed in lines face down on the desk. One is the fortune teller, the other child chooses a card. The fortune teller picks it up without showing it, looks at the drawing in the crystal ball and with a suitably mysterious voice says *I can see a (star).* The 'fortune teller' then reads the sentence written below *You are going to (be famous)!* Each child can choose five cards. When they change over, the cards must be shuffled again.

HOME AGAIN!

Lesson 3

OBJECTIVES:	to discriminate between descriptions; to recognise the use of emphasis
RECYCLED LANGUAGE:	describing people
MATERIALS:	cassette recorder, cassette 2, photocopies of resource page 158

9 Listen and complete. Read and match.

1 Focus attention on the picture of Ben and Kanda. Give the children a few moments to study the exchange and then ask why they think Ben and Kanda are pointing at each other. Ben is telling Kanda *You are an alien!* and Kanda replies with *You are an alien!*

2 Let the children listen to the tape, and then repeat the dialogue.

3 Focus attention on the significance of the change in stress and on the relative concept of *alien*.

4 Ask the children if they know any films with alien characters and what their names are. Focus attention on the photos and ask them if they recognise any of the films or if they've seen any of them. Discuss the role of the aliens in one of the films.

5 Tell the children they are going to listen to descriptions of three of these. Once the aliens have been identified, focus attention on the gapped descriptions and tell the children they are going to listen again and that this time they have to fill in the missing words. All the missing words are shown around the corresponding photos. Stop the tape where necessary to give them time to write.

Tapescript and key
One
ET is an alien in a very famous *film*. He's from a distant *planet*. He's *smaller* than a man, he's got a big head and big *blue* eyes. He's got short legs and *long* arms. He can fly on a bike! He *must* send a message to go home.
Two
Chewbacca is an alien in *Star Wars*. He's a *pilot*. He's very tall, *strong* and hairy. He's *always* hungry! He *can't* speak. He *doesn't* like Darth Vader.
Three
Jabba is another alien in Star Wars. He's very *big* and fat. He's nasty, *slimy* and clever. He always eats *frogs*. He *never* walks. He's got a pet *monster* called Bantha.

6 Check by reading out the passage, stopping at the gaps and letting the children say the word they have written. Ask them comprehension-check questions including questions that require an *I don't know* answer, e.g. *Where's ET/Chewbacca from? (A distant planet.) Is ET taller than me? What can he do? How many legs has he got? Is he hairy/fat/slimy/nasty/strong,* etc? *Does he like ...? Does he (walk)? (Never),* etc.

Escape door: space stories

1 This activity leads to a funny nonsense story in which, by asking the children to write a word without knowing the context, they discover they have produced an amusing story. Hand out photocopies of the Space Story on resource page 158.

2 Focus attention on the numbered lines on the page and using the instructions and hints below, help them to complete them.

1 Make up and write a very strange name. (*Parox, Jovee, Crave,* etc.)
2 Write the name of something from the landscape. Make it plural. (*trees, lakes,* etc.)
3 Write a word that describes the temperature. (*hot, cold, warm*)
4 Add the letters *-ians* to your very strange name and write it here. (*Paroxians*)
5 Write a colour.
6 Write a word to describe someone. (*tall, short, thin, fat, strong, weak, nice, nasty,* etc.)
7 Write another word of the same kind.
8 Write a number from two to ten.
9 Write a part of the body. Make it plural.
10 Write an activity. (*play football, go shopping, sleep, have a shower, collect litter,* etc.)
11 Write another activity of the same kind.
12 Write an activity/action. (*jump, run, walk, sleep, climb ropes, work outside/inside,* etc.)
13 Write another activity/action.
14 Write a word describing a feeling. (*happy, sad, tired, hungry, angry, thirsty, bored,* etc.)
15 Write a sentence (any complete sentence or expression).
16 Write a word describing a feeling. (*happy, sad, tired, hungry, angry, thirsty, bored,* etc)
17 Write a sentence (any complete sentence or expression).
18 Make up and write another strange name.
19 Add *-ians* to this new name.

i **FACILITATING THE TASK: some of the group words are very straightforward, e.g. *Choose a colour.* Others are slightly more challenging. If you feel that your class would find it too stretching to do the activity spontaneously, elicit acceptable words/expressions for each instruction before doing the activity and write them on the board so the children can choose one. Some have been given by way of example. Remind the children of previously studied language.**

3 When they have finished, choose one of the silliest and read it to the class, underlining by your intonation and expressions the amusing sections.

4 Give the children time to read their own stories and ask them to read out to the class the sections they find most amusing. They can also illustrate any part of the story.

Key (Sample nonsense story)

(Parox) is a small planet in a distant solar system. There are lots of *(stones)* on *(Parox)* and it is a very *(hot)* planet. *(Paroxians)* are *(blue)*. They're *(tall)* and *(strong)* and they've got *(six)* legs and three *(eyes)*. They must *(go shopping)* at night and *(sleep)* during the day. They never *(go to school)* and they always *(jump)*. They speak a very strange language. When a *(Paroxian)* is very *(happy)* he always says *(I've got a dog)*, and when he is *(angry)* he says *(Can you give me a rucksack?)*.

(Paroxians) have magic *(stones)*. These *(stones)* can make them invisible.

One day, aliens from *(Antor)* attack *(Parox)*; when they arrive they can't see the *(Paroxians)* because they are invisible, but they can hear voices all around. The *(Antorians)* think that *(Parox)* is full of ghosts and they run away.

HOME AGAIN!

Extension: choose and mime

Choose one of the stories at random. Read the story through once. Tell the children you are going to read it again and this time they have to mime the story as you read it out. Highlight the sections to be mimed and give them time to carry out the actions, e.g. *When they are angry, they always say 'My brother is stupid'.*

Extension: group project

Divide the children into four groups and tell them each group is part of a film crew involved in a new science fiction film. Introduce *science fiction* in English. Each group has to deal with one aspect of the film. The four tasks are:

Group 1 Write a list of rules for the inhabitants of the planet. *They must/mustn't ... .*

Group 2 Describe the landscape on the planet. *It's big/hot/cold. There are lakes/trees,* etc.

Group 3 Write what the inhabitants are like (or choose one of the versions already done in the previous activity) and what they can/can't do. *They can/can't fly/speak,* etc.

Group 4 Describe a good animal and a nasty animal that live on the planet.

Each group, as well as writing a description, has to produce a picture that illustrates what they have written. When the groups have finished they cut out the elements and stick them on the landscape background. Stick the written descriptions around the scene.

Lesson 4

OBJECTIVES:	to make/accept/reject suggestions; to talk about films and videos
TARGET LANGUAGE:	*What shall we do/watch? Let's watch ... ,* types of films (*comedy, western, action, adventure, science fiction, cartoon, documentary*)
RECYCLED LANGUAGE:	*Good idea! I like/don't like ... .*
MATERIALS:	cassette recorder, cassette 2, photocopies of resource page 158

Introduction

1 Focus attention on the films on page 88. Ask the class *What kind of film is it? (science fiction). Do you like science fiction films?* Elicit examples of science fiction films.
2 Elicit other kinds of films using film characters as prompts, e.g. Hercules and Jumanji are characters in adventure/action films. Introduce these words in English. Most of the other kinds of films, e.g. *western, thriller, horror films, cartoons, documentaries* should already be familiar from previous work or from *Quest* 2.
3 Ask them if the cinema is the only place they can watch a film. (*No, you can watch a video.*) Ask if they have a video player at home, if they rent videos or if they have a video collection.

10 Listen and tick.

1 Ask the children to look at the two boys in the first drawing in Activity 10. Ask what the problem is (*He's bored*) and what the suggestion is (*Let's watch a video*).

2 Focus attention on the grid and tell the children they are going to listen to the two boys, James and Jack, talking about the films and deciding which film they want to see.

3 The first task for the children is to find out and tick which category each film belongs to.

4 The children listen again and, using the grid, identify which films James and Jack like/don't like by putting ticks or crosses in the appropriate column.

Tapescript

James	I'm bored! What shall we do?
Jack	Let's watch a video!
James	Good idea! Wow! You've got a lot of videos!
Jack	Yes, this is my Dad's video library. We often watch videos. Which film do you want to see?
James	... Errr ... Let's watch *Rambo*. It's a fantastic film!
Jack	Mmmm, *Rambo* is an action film and I don't like action films ... and *Rambo* is horrible! Look at this ... I like this: *Jumanji!* Let's watch *Jumanji!*
James	Hmmm ... I like adventure films, but I don't like *Jumanji* ... there are spiders ... I'm afraid of spiders.
Jack	But it's just a film! OK, let's see ... do you want to see *Star Wars?* It's a great science fiction film!
James	Well, I like science fiction films, but I don't want to watch *Star Wars* ...
Jack	Here's a documentary on volcanoes! Wow! I like documentaries. Let's watch *Volcanoes.*
James	*Volcanoes?* Mmmm ... I don't want to watch that ... my Dad always watches it!
Jack	It's a bit difficult ... what's this? Bud Spencer? ... Oh no! I don't like comedy films. They're stupid!
James	OK. Here's a cartoon! *Hercules.*
Jack	Great! I like cartoons and *Hercules* is my favourite.
James	I like it too. Let's watch *Hercules!*

11 Work in pairs.

1 Photocopy resource page 158 and put the children in pairs.

2 Give out the film cards telling the children not to show them to their partners.

3 The first task is to write the name of a film belonging to each category. They can choose any film they like even if the title is in L1. To do this the children take it in turns and then they both write the title in the space provided, e.g.

A *Tell me the name of a science fiction film!*

B *Independence Day.*

They both write *Independence Day* in the space on the card.

B *Tell me the name ...* etc.

RE-USING THE ACTIVITY: if you tell the children to write the titles in pencil, the cards can be used again, with different titles every time you do the activity.

4 The second task is to decide together which film to see. Focus attention on the faces next to the film types and explain that the faces tell them if they like the film type or not. They must answer according to the face and not their own opinion at this stage. They follow the dialogue model on the board:

HOME AGAIN!

A *What shall we do?*
B *Let's watch a video!*
A *Yes, let's watch (Independence Day)!*
B *No, I don't like science fiction films. Let's watch Bud Spencer!*
A *Hmm. I don't like comedy films. Let's watch a documentary ... , etc.*
B *Let's watch Tom and Jerry!*
A *Yes, good idea. I like cartoons!*

Extension: choose your own!

The second row of faces allows a personalisation of the activity. The children do the activity again expressing their real opinion about the films.

Drama time

11 Home Again! (See page 10 of the Introduction for notes on *Drama time* for the story.)

12 REVISION

> OBJECTIVES: to revise the language presented in Units 9 – 11
> MATERIALS: cassette player, cassette 2, photocopies of resource page 159

Introduction

Ask the children if they sometimes go to the cinema, how long a film lasts, how many shows a day there are, how much it costs, and ask them if the cinema they usually go to is big or small; explain that there are some cinemas which have several screens and which show three or four (or more) films at the same time in different rooms.

1 Read and answer.

1 Focus attention on the posters at the top of the page. Ask them which films are showing. (*Hercules, Jumanji* and *101 Dalmatians*) and what information is given on them (*name of film, days showing, dates, times, actors,* etc).

2 Focus attention on the two tickets and ask the children what they are and what information is shown on them.

3 The children read the questions and answer them, writing their answers in the appropriate spaces. Point out that some of the information they will be able to deduce from the posters, other information is explicit.

4 When they have finished, ask them to check their answers in pairs then go through the questions one at a time.

Key

1 *101 Dalmatians*   2 all of the films   3 Yes
4 *101 Dalmatians*   5 £8.50   6 No
7 Each film lasts 2 hours so you can see *101 Dalmatians* first and then *Hercules*.
8 Yes   9 *101 Dalmatians*   10 *Hercules*

2 Doctor Alpha's robot

1 Explain that Doctor Alpha is having problems with his new talking robot. The robot has said several sentences and he must examine the sentences to see which are logical and which are not. Write these sentences on the board and ask the children to read them.

Ben is reading a chicken.   *I have geography on Thursdays.*
This ice cream costs £500.00.   *Bats can't fly.*
There's a schoolbag in my pencil case. *This is my sister. His name's Julie.*
You mustn't run in the swimming pool. *North is opposite South.*

2 Now ask the children to correct the sentences they think are not logical.

3 SONG: The Prince of Arion

See page 15 of the Introduction for more suggestions on dealing with songs and raps.

1 Hand out copies of resource page 159. Let the children read the words of the song and look at the pictures.

2 Teach them the song in the usual way, then, when they are confident with the words, let them sing.

REVISION

| OBJECTIVES: | to revise the language presented in Units 9–11 |
| MATERIALS: | dice, counter, photocopies of resource page 160 |

4 GAME: Tunnel game

See page 15 of the Introduction for more suggestions on dealing with games.

1   This simple board game can be played in pairs or in small groups. Hand out copies of resource page 160. To play the children will need a counter for each player and one dice.

2   Explain the rules of the game, which are as follows:

    a   the children take it in turns to move according to the number thrown on the dice.

    b   when a player lands on a square he/she must answer the question or perform the task required on the corresponding square on the photocopy of the resource page.

    c   if this is done correctly he/she may proceed to his/her next turn. If not, he/she misses a turn.

    d   if a player lands on a tunnel square, he/she must answer both the questions on the connected squares.

    e   if these are answered correctly the player may go through the tunnel. If not, the player remains on the first square and must proceed along the board.

5 Put the sentences in order.

Write some sentences on the board in a jumbled order. The children must write the sentences in the correct word order in their exercise books. Here are some suggestions:

My father is a policeman.	*Toby doesn't like comedy films.*	*What are you going to do?*
The bank is opposite the school.	*Susan is taller than Toby.*	*What shall we do?*
I was at the cinema yesterday.	*I always get up at seven o'clock.*	*How much is it?*

6 Quest Quiz

1   The class is divided into two or four teams which play against each other. The children in each team have to produce ten questions based on the *Quest* story pages. They decide on the questions and then write them on a sheet of paper.

2   When all ten questions are ready, check them for mistakes. Give the team 2 points for each correct question, 1 point if it contains just spelling mistakes and 0 points if there is a lot wrong! Let the children correct any mistakes.

3   When both teams are ready, give the question paper to the opposing team. The first team to answer all the questions calls out *Finished!* and the game stops. Check the answers of both teams. Give 2 points for a correct answer or, at your discretion, 1 point if the sentence is correct but contains a spelling mistake. The questions may refer to either the *Quest* characters and the story, and/or information related to the children themselves.

Storyboard

See page 11 of the Introduction for notes on the *Storyboard*.

Divide the class into small groups. Get each group to draw the principal scenes from the story in Units 9, 10 and 11. This session of the *Storyboard* will complete the wall frieze. See the notes in Unit 4 Lesson 2 page 50 for details of how to handle the session.

Summer holiday scene

Special Dates

Song: Kanda

A lonely spaceship
Out in space.
The solar system's
A lonely place.
Neptune, Jupiter, Saturn and Mars
Mercury, Pluto, Venus, the stars.

Kanda, Prince Kanda!
Where are you?
Kanda, Prince Kanda!
This planet is new.
Kanda, Prince Kanda!
Earth's green and blue.
Kanda, Prince Kanda!
Damek Za ... is after you! (twice)

Listen and find
the missing planet.

UNIT 1 LESSON 4

Life on a spaceship

What's number 1?
You can sleep here. ....

You can speak to your friends on Earth, because there's a telephone.
What number is it? ....

If you don't want to fly, put on your special shoes.
They are number ....

There isn't a bathroom, but you can have a shower here.
It's number ....

You can't ride your bike in space, but there's a gym.
Where is it? ....

From a window you can take a photo of the moon and the Earth.
What number is it? ....

What's number 5? ....

There's a kitchen. It's very small, but you can eat special food.
What number is it? ....

Drinking is difficult in space, but you can have a special coke!
Who's drinking it? ....

You can go to the toilet, but put on the belts!

Where's the toilet? ....

Map of Europe

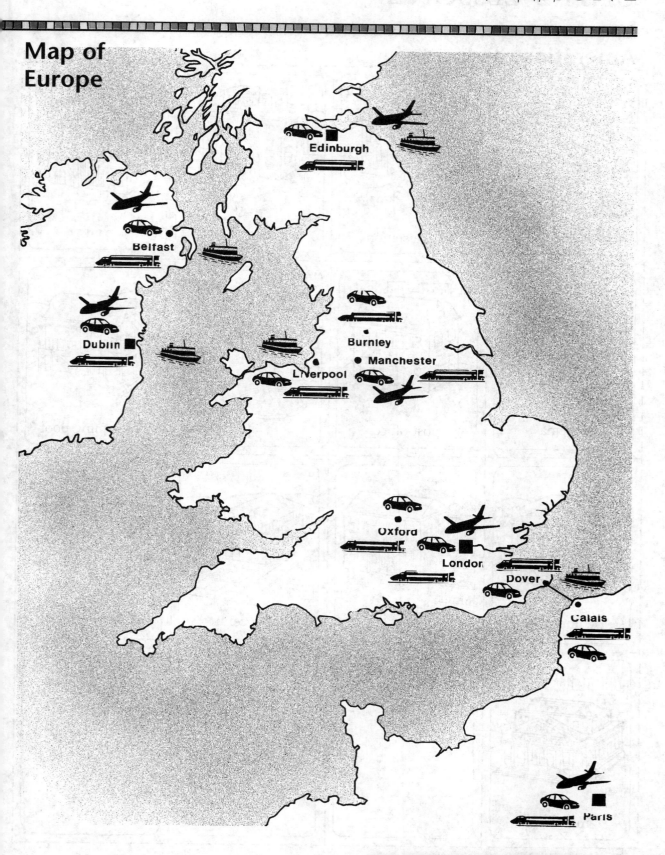

UNIT 2 LESSON 2

Amenities cards

bus stop	police station	hospital	bank
cinema	post office	park	swimming pool
library	school	sports centre	amusement arcade
museum			

Place cards

Kidston

a police station

a hospital

a bank

a supermarket

a hamburger bar

a museum

a cinema

a post office

a park

a swimming pool

a library

a school

a sports centre

an amusement arcade

a toy shop

UNIT 2 LESSON 3

Place cards (continued)

Song: The Line Rap

One step forward
Face your partner
Clap your hands and
Back behind the line.

Go straight on - one
Go straight on - two
Hands together and
Back behind the line.

Rap it! Rap it!
You can sing it or tap it!
Rap it! Rap it!
Do what you want but
Back behind the line!

Turn round quickly
Step back slowly
Turn left, turn right
Back behind the line.

Rap it! Rap it!
You can sing it or tap it!
Rap it! Rap it!
Do what you want but
Back behind the line!

Sing and dance.
Look and match.

London Maps

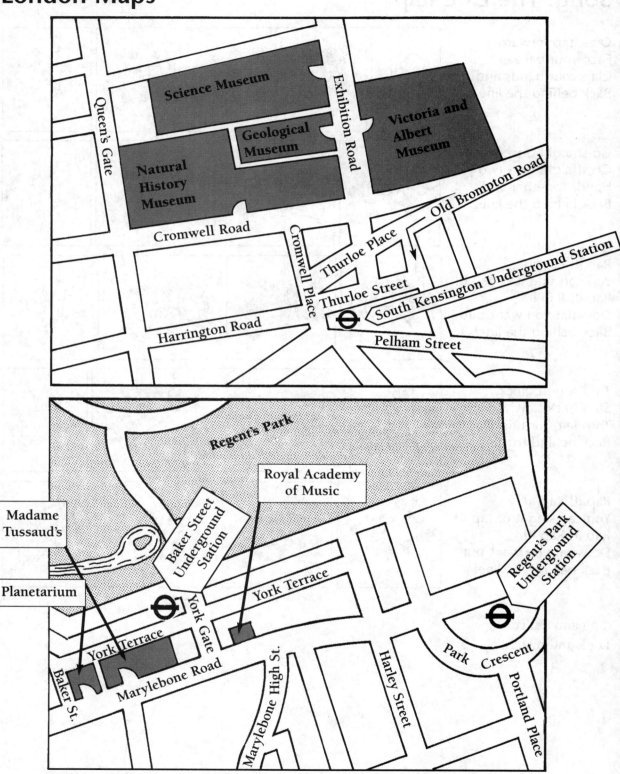

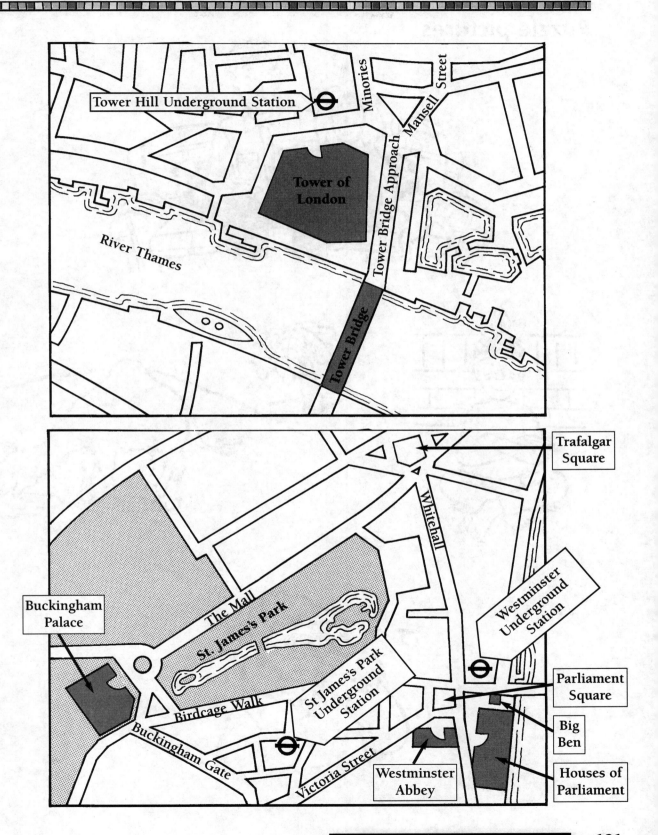

Puzzle pictures

Song: Luna

Deep beneath the light blue water
Hidden where no-one can see her
Luna the mermaid sings her magic spell.
She wants to be Princess Mary
A queen or bird or magic fairy.
She wants to live near a lake
Or near a wishing-well.

Every day she plays her violin
Every night she's ready to sing.

The wind is blowing
The tide is flowing
And there is no way of knowing
When Luna the mermaid
Will see her wish come true.

What does Luna want to be?

UNIT 4 LESSON 2

Game: The golden planet cards

Where's the cinema?

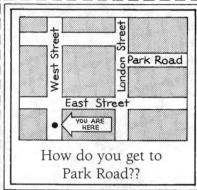

How do you get to
Park Road??

What's this?

Who are they?

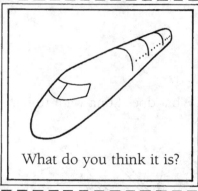

What do you think it is?

How do you get
to London?

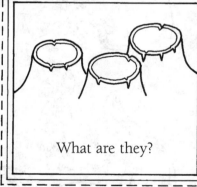

What are they?

What are they?

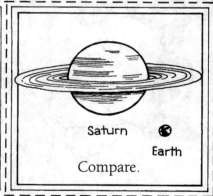

Compare.

Who's the tallest?

Is the Police Station
next to the Museum?

Excuse me. Where's the
swimming pool?

Game: The golden planet cards (continued)

Ask a question starting with *What?*

What's this?

Compare.

You want to buy ... . Complete.

What's he saying?

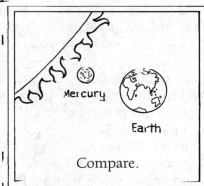

Compare.

Where's the museum?

What's she saying?

Ask a question starting with *Where?*

What's this?

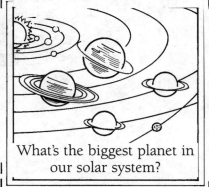

What's the biggest planet in our solar system?

Damek Za wants to kill Kanda. Why?

UNIT 4 LESSON 2

Song: My home town

I can see my house
Near the school.
I remember running to
The swimming pool
I can see the square
And my uncle's bar.
I remember all the shops
And where they are ...

I like it! I like it! I really do!
I like it! I like it! And so will you ...
I like it! I like it! I like it! You know?
I like it! I like it! I like it! Let's go!
Let's go ... to my home town!

I can see the church
And the river too.
I remember playing in
The park with Sue.
I can see the fields
And the sky so blue.
I remember all the things
I want to show you.

I like it! I like it! I really do!
I like it! I like it! And so will you ...
I like it! I like it! I like it! You know?
I like it! I like it! I like it! Let's go!
Let's go ... to my home town!

Look, listen and choose.

136 © **Pearson Education . Photocopiable**

English money

UNIT 5 LESSON 3

Where's Mum?

Where's Mum?
Where's Mum?
She's here somewhere
She's shopping in town
Let's try in there!

The (baker's) nice.
Let me see your list.
I haven't got these
I haven't got this.
I'd like some (bread).
Yes, here you are.
Try the next shop.
Mum won't be far.

Where's Mum?
Where's Mum?
She's here somewhere
She's shopping in town
Let's try in there!

The (greengrocer's) nice.
Let me see your list.
I haven't got these
I haven't got this.
I'd like some (pears).
Yes, here you are.
Try the next shop.
Mum won't be far.

Where's Mum?
Where's Mum?
She's here somewhere
She's shopping in town
Let's try in there!

Listen and tick.
Look at the shopping list and continue the song.

Camping cards

tent

sleeping bag

blanket

UNIT 6 LESSON 2

Camping cards (continued)

toilet paper	towel	soap
pan	cup	plate
knife	fork	spoon

Song: Camping

Let's go camping
Let's go camping
by the sea or near a mountain.
Let's go camping
Let's go camping.
We're jumping in the car!
Let's go!

John's lighting a fire
Meg's climbing a tree
Joe's swimming in the river
He's waving at me.

Let's go camping ...

Pam's going for a walk
Bob's washing a dish
Sally's in the water
Trying to catch a fish.

Let's go camping ...

Sue is always hungry
She's looking for a plate
Jimmy is the smallest one
He always wants to play.

Let's go camping ...

Who is who? Listen and write.

Safari Park dialogue

Listen and fill in the missing words.

Mr. Robbins	Right. Here we are.
Kids	Hooray!
Mr. Robbins	Let's look at the .... Mmm. What .... first?
Kids	I want to see the lions/snakes/bears!
Mr. Robbins	Sssshh! Listen. We've got two hours. We can't see all the animals.
Kids	Oh, no! What a pity!
Mr. Robbins	Now, let's see. Tell me, what .... to see, Tommy?
Tommy	I want to see the .... and those enormous .... and ...
Silvy	Yuuuukkkk!!
Mr. Robbins	And you, Silvy?
Silvy	I'd like to see the ....
David	And I want to see the snakes.
Mr. Robbins	Mmm. They're in different areas. .... ?
Silvy	Well, all right. Let's see your horrible .... and crocodiles ...
David	... then, ... the black panthers ...

Song: Stunt lady

She jumps through fire
She fights a lion
She jumps from a plane
Then nobody knows
where Danji goes
Nobody knows
what Danji knows.

Stunt lady
Half crazy
I want to be like you!
Stunt lady
Half crazy
I want to be like you!

She runs so fast
She's never last
She gets there just in time.
Then nobody knows
where Danji goes
Nobody knows
what Danji knows.

She's an action star
In a new sports car
She always stops the crime.
Then nobody knows
where Danji goes
Nobody knows
what Danji knows.

Stunt lady
Half crazy
I want to be like you!
Stunt lady
Half crazy
I want to be like you!

Listen and number.

UNIT 8 LESSON 1

Word hunt

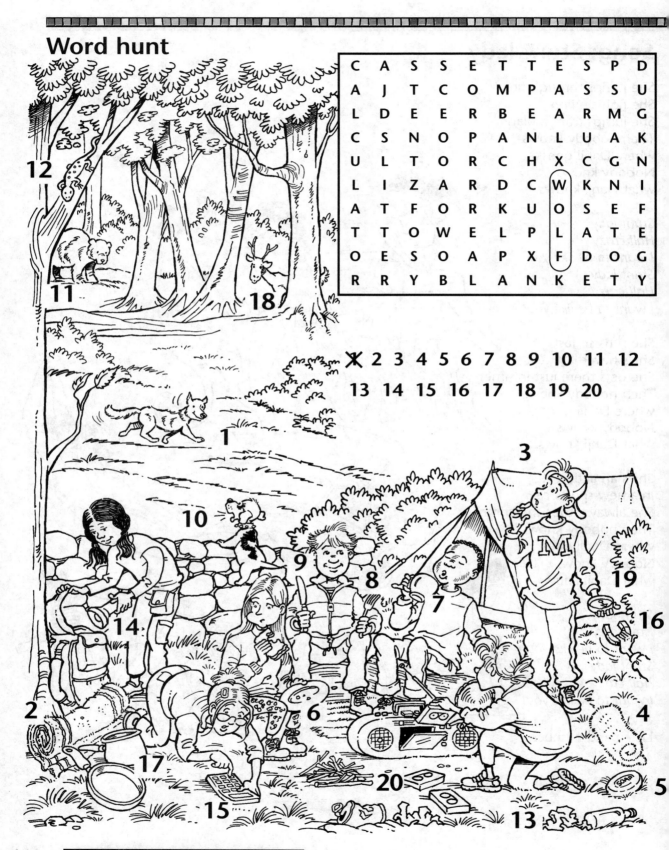

C	A	S	S	E	T	T	E	S	P	D
A	J	T	C	O	M	P	A	S	S	U
L	D	E	E	R	B	E	A	R	M	G
C	S	N	O	P	A	N	L	U	A	K
U	L	T	O	R	C	H	X	C	G	N
L	I	Z	A	R	D	C	W	K	N	I
A	T	F	O	R	K	U	O	S	E	F
T	T	O	W	E	L	P	L	A	T	E
O	E	S	O	A	P	X	F	D	O	G
R	R	Y	B	L	A	N	K	E	T	Y

X 2 3 4 5 6 7 8 9 10 11 12
13 14 15 16 17 18 19 20

Sentence snake

UNIT 8 LESSON 2

Game: Job Cluedo

policeman
1 He wears a uniform.
2 He drives a car.
3 He checks documents.

shop assistant
1 She works during the day.
2 She works inside.
3 She sells toys.

bus driver
1 wears a uniform.
2 Sometimes she works at night.
3 She drives a bus.

clerk
1 He works during the day.
2 He works inside.
3 He checks documents.

ticket inspector
1 Sometimes he works at night.
2 He wears a uniform.
3 He checks tickets.

pilot
1 He wears a uniform.
2 He travels around the world.
3 He flies planes.

park ranger
1 He wears a uniform.
2 He drives a jeep.
3 He travels round the park.

chemist
1 Sometimes she works at night.
2 She works inside.
3 She sells medicines.

Song: Spider

spiders ... spiders ... spiders ... spiders ...

Are you afraid of spiders?
Are you afraid of spiders?
If you're not afraid of spiders
Touch one if you can!

Spiders, snakes, boats and planes
Scorpions, bats, ships and trains
I'm not afraid of anything
I'm not afraid at all!

snakes ... snakes ... snakes ... snakes ...

Are you afraid of snakes?
Are you afraid of snakes?
If you're not afraid of snakes
Touch one if you can!

Spiders, snakes, boats and planes
Scorpions, bats, ships and trains
I'm not afraid of anything
I'm not afraid at all!

?? ... ?? ... ?? ... ?? ...

Are you afraid of ... ?
Are you afraid of ... ?
If you're not afraid of ...
Touch one if you can!

Spiders, snakes, boats and planes
Scorpions, bats, ships and trains
I'm not afraid of anything
I'm not afraid at all!

Sing and mime.

UNIT 9 LESSON 2

Animal descriptions

Black Widow Spider	Megabat	Anaconda
This spider is not very big, but it is dangerous and very poisonous. It eats small animals and insects. Sometimes it attacks man when disturbed, and its bite can kill you. It lives in North America and South America and likes warm, wet places.	It's the biggest bat in the world. Sometimes its wingspan can be 1.7 metres. It isn't poisonous or dangerous, and it doesn't attack man or animals because it eats fruit. It likes warm, wet places, and it lives in trees in the jungles of Java.	It's the longest and strongest snake in the world, and it can be 10 metres long! It eats small animals by squeezing them. The anaconda isn't poisonous. Sometimes it eats big animals too - it can eat a pig! It lives in the forests of South America and generally it doesn't attack man.

UNIT 9 LESSON 4

Personality questionnaire

Do you ever ...

	Yes: always	Yes: often	Yes: sometimes	No: never
get up early on Sundays?				
do your homework?				
help at home?				
go to the shops?				
have a party on your birthday?				
go camping?				
watch TV?				

Write about your friend.

(name of friend) .... gets up early on Sundays.
He/She .... does his/her homework.
.... helps at home.
.... goes to the ....
.... has a .... his/her birthday.
.... camping.
.... watches ....

Funfair

UNIT 10 LESSON 1

Speech bubbles

Song: Fly!

Boy	Oh! What's the code?
Girl	Here ... six ... three ... seven ... eight ... double O ... nine ... . There!
Both	Yeeeesssss!!!

6 - 3 - 7 - 8 - double 0 - 9
It's the only way to go!
6 - 3 - 7 - 8 - double 0 - 9
It's time to start the show!

Take me flying high on
a roller coaster
Take me flying high in the sky
Take me flying down through a long
dark tunnel
Over the bridge and fly, fly, fly!

6 - 3 - 7 - 8 - double 0 - 9
It's the only way to go!
6 - 3 - 7 - 8 - double 0 - 9
It's time to start the show!

Fly above the trees like a golden eagle
Round and round like a Big Wheel
Up and down the mountain,
through the forest
On our wings of steel,
wings of steel!

Sing and mime.

Song: Nothing

You mustn't run
You mustn't fight
You mustn't read in the dark
Or stay up all night.
What can I do?
... Nothing!

You mustn't jump
You mustn't talk
You mustn't eat
in the swimming pool
And you must walk!
What can I do?
... Nothing!

*If we go to the
swimming pool
or go to school
If we go to
the cinema
It's rules, rules, rules!
What can we do?
... Nothing!*

Sing and mime.

Place game cards

UNIT 10 LESSON 4

Time/Question game cards

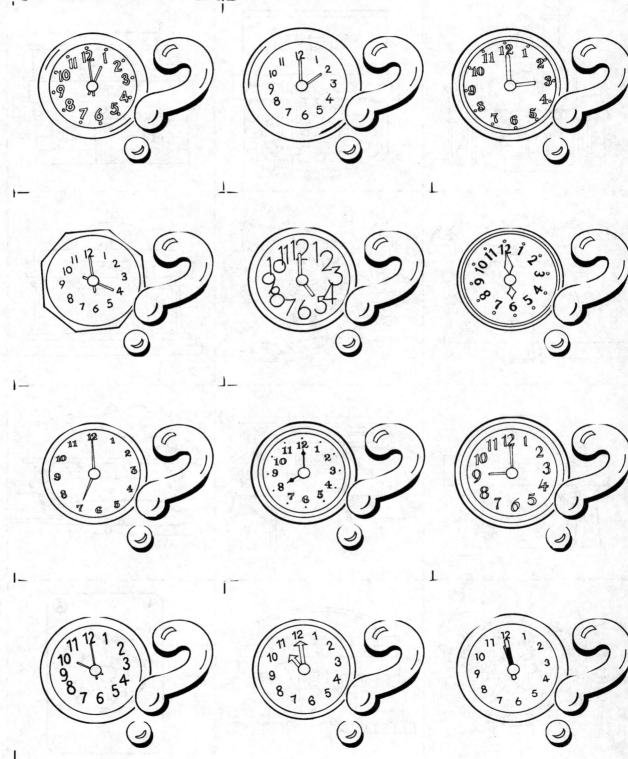

Song: Holiday rap

Where are you going to spend your holidays?
France or England, Greece or Spain?
How are you going to get there, Susan?
Car or coach or ship or plane?

I'm going to see some very old places
I'm going to buy a ticket too
I'm going to leave from London Airport
I'm going to go where the sea is blue!

What are you going to do there, Susan?
Play or study, or cycle or swim?
What are you going to take there, Susan?

Surfboard, camera, bike or pen?
I'm going to cycle round the village
I'm going to swim in the swimming pool
I'm going to take a lot of photos
I'm going to write a letter to you!

Where are you going to spend your holidays?
What are you going to take with you?
How are you going to get there, Susan?
And then what are you going to do?

Listen and guess.

155

UNIT 11 LESSON 2

Holiday scenes and cutouts

Fortune telling cards

You're going to be famous.

You're going to be a doctor.

You're going to live in a castle.

You're going to work in America.

You're going to have five children.

You're going to travel around the world.

You're going to visit the moon.

You're going to travel in space.

You're going to marry a monkey.

You're going to work with a computer.

You're going to make a film called the Big Banana.

You're going to write a book.

You're going to have twenty pets.

You're going to spend your holidays in Africa.

You're going to meet the President of America.

You're going to play the violin.

UNIT 11 LESSON 3

Space story

1 ....   is a small planet in a distant solar system. There are lots of
2 ....   on 1 ....   and it is a very
3 ....   planet. 4 ....   are
5 .... They're 6 ....   and
7 ....   and they've got 8 ....   legs and three
9 .... They must 10 ....   at night and
11 ....   during the day. They never 12 ....   and
they always 13 .... They speak a very strange language. When
4 ....   are very 14 ....   they always say
15 ....   , and when they are 16 ....   they say
17 .... 4 ....   have magic
2 .... These 2 ....   can make them invisible.
One day, aliens from 18 ....   attack 1 ....   ;
when they arrive they can't see the 4 ....   because they are invisible,
but they can hear voices all around. The 19 ....   think that
1 ....   is full of ghosts and they run away.

UNIT 11 LESSON 4

Film cards

Science fiction film	☺	☺	**Science fiction film**	☹ ☺
Comedy film	☹	☺	**Comedy film**	☺ ☺
Documentary	☺	☺	**Documentary**	☹ ☺
Action film	☺	☺	**Action film**	☹ ☺
Horror film	☹	☺	**Horror film**	☺ ☺
Cartoon	☺	☺	**Cartoon**	☺ ☺

Song: Prince of Arion

When I see a star
I'll think of you
Who you are
And what you do.

Across the years
In deepest space
I remember you
I see your face.

Where were you
When danger was near?
Where were you
When the night was clear?

I can see it all again.
I was the prince
The prince of Arion.

I was in the dark
I was far from home
I was in the park
I was all alone.

UNIT 12 LESSON 2

Game: Tunnel game

1 Name three planets.	**2** Say a rule with *mustn't*.	**3** Compare Pluto and Mars.	**4** Name three things for camping.
8 Who is the biggest?	**7** How do you get to the house?	**6** Sing a song in English.	**5** What's the name of the king of Arion?
9 Do you live in a city, a town or a village?	**10** Say a rule with *must*.	**11** How much is it?	**12** How do you say these in English?
16 What are these?	**15** What are you afraid of?	**14** What are these?	**13** Name four shops
17 Where's the Post Office?	**18** How do you get to the school?	**19** What do you think it is?	**20** Say a rule with *mustn't*.
24 What's the name of Rui's brother?	**23** Where were you yesterday at four o'clock?	**22** Say a sentence with *always*.	**21** What are they doing?
25 Say a sentence with *never*.	**26** Where are you going to spend your holidays?	**27** What's his job?	**28** What kind of films do you like?